THE
RATIONALE
OF
LEGAL
PUNISHMENT

THE
RATIONALE
OF
LEGAL
PUNISHMENT

EDMUND L. PINCOFFS
Associate Professor of Philosophy
University of Texas

1966
HUMANITIES PRESS
New York

© Copyright 1966 by
HUMANITIES PRESS, INC.
New York, N. Y. 10010

Library of Congress Catalog Card Number 66-20334

Printed in the United States of America

This Book is Dedicated to the Memory
of my Father,

EDMUND PETER PINCOFFS

He asked a very simple question: "Why, and by what right, do some people lock up, torment, exile, flog, and kill others, while they are themselves just like those they torment, flog, and kill?" And in answer he got delibertions as to whether human beings had free-will or not; whether or not signs of criminality could be detected by measuring the skull; what part heredity played in crime; whether immorality could be inherited; and what madness is, what degeneration is, and what temperament is; how climate, food, ignorance, imitativeness, hypnotism, or passion affect crime; what society is, what its duties are—and so on . . . , but there was no answer on the chief point: "By what right do some people punish others?"

LEO TOLSTOY, *Resurrection*

PREFACE

To all philosophical conversationalists, correspondents, and readers who have goaded and guided me in the preparation of this book, Thanks! I should especially mention John Rawls, Stuart Brown, Norman Malcolm, Jerome Hall, Gregory Vlastos, and Joel Feinberg.

My thanks are also due to Princeton University and the Firestone Library for carrel and quiet during my year as Visiting Fellow, in 1962-63; and to the University of Houston for leave-of-absence.

Finally, my thanks go to Mary Elizabeth Pincoffs for her forbearance and her encouragement. Without these crutches, the author might never have hobbled into print.

TABLE OF CONTENTS

THE
RATIONALE
OF
LEGAL
PUNISHMENT

THE CLASSICAL DEBATE

If it were done when 'tis done, then 'twere well
It were done quickly. If the assassination
Could trammel up the consequence, and catch
With his surcease, success; that but this blow
Might be the be-all and the end-all here,
But here, upon this bank and shoal of time,
We'ld jump the life to come. But in these cases
We still have judgment here; that we but teach
Bloody instructions, which being taught return
To plague th' inventor. This even-handed justice
Commends th' ingredients of our poisoned chalice
To our own lips.

SHAKESPEARE, Macbeth

Punishment has in it the notion of a remedy, and
has the place of a mean, not of an end.

BENJAMIN WHICHCOTE, *Moral and Religious Aphorisms*

Legal punishment is viewed by some of the most sensitive and well-educated people of our time as a survival of barbarism, bereft of rational foundation, supported only by inertia and the wish to have vengeance on criminals. In this book, I shall be concerned solely with the rational foundations of punishment; not with its history, sociology, or psychology. I shall argue that though the question concerning the grounds of punishment is indeed vexed and confused, there are grounds; and that he who would substitute some other practice for punishment should be aware of them.

If the confusion concerning the foundations, or grounds, or rationale (I use the terms synonymously) of punishment is to be removed, a famous theoretical impasse must be examined in detail: the impasse between the retributivistic and the utilitarian positions. This will be the first order of business. What the critics of legal punishment have suspected, I hope to show more precisely: that the traditional theories are contraries. More seriously, neither theory is alone adequate to provide a satisfactory rationale for punishment. And, more seriously yet, modern attempts to show that the contrariety is merely apparent, arising out of failure to distinguish different levels of punishment-justification, fail. The second order of business consists in an attempted reconstruction of the rationale of punishment.

I hope that it will be apparent that my intention is not to carry on a polemic against retributivists, utilitarians, skeptics who despair of finding rational grounds, or humanitarians who rejoice in finding none. It is, rather, understanding and a carefully reasoned stance. It should be apparent that the human stakes are too high to wager on the outcome of professorial jousting matches.

In this chapter, I attempt to reconstruct the traditional retributivist position: the position held by Kant, Hegel, and Bradley; and the traditional ultilitarian position, as expounded by Paley and Bentham. Modern readers have much more difficulty understanding (not merely agreeing with) the retributive view than the utilitarian one.[1] Thus, I devote far more space to it. This explanation of the opposing views is examined in Chapter II, where the chief arguments in the age-old debate are examined; and in Chapters IV and V, where the implications for judicial procedure and legislation are traced out. Chapter III is an attempt to sort out some of the main issues in the arguments over the rationale of punishment, Chapter VI takes up the proposed substitution of treatment for punishment, and VII offers a qualified defense of the practice of legal punishment. Those readers who are familiar with the historical debate would do well to proceed directly to the second Chapter.

I

The classification of Kant as a retributivist is usually accompanied by a reference to some part of the following passage from the *Rechtslehre*, which is worth quoting at length.

Juridical punishment can never be administered merely as a means for promoting another good either with regard to the criminal himself or to civil society, but must in all cases be imposed only because the individual on whom it is inflicted *has committed a crime*. For one man ought never to be dealt with merely as a means subservient to the purpose of another, nor be mixed up with the subjects of real right. Against such treatment his inborn personality has a right to protect him, even although he may be condemned to lose his civil personality. He must first be found guilty and *punishable* before there can be any thought of drawing from his punishment any benefit for himself or his fellow-citizens. The penal law is a categorical imperative; and woe to him who creeps through the serpent-windings of utilitarianism to discover some advantage that may discharge him from the justice of punishment, or even from the due measure of it, according to the Pharisaic maxim: "It is better that *one* man should die than the whole people should perish." For if justice and righteousness perish, human life would no longer have any value in the world. . . .

But what is the mode and measure of punishment which public justice takes as its principle and standard? It is just the principle of equality, by which the pointer of the scale of justice is made to incline no more to the one side than the other. It may be rendered by saying that the undeserved evil which any one commits on another, is to be regarded as perpetrated on himself. Hence it may be said: "If you slander another, you slander yourself; if you steal from another, you steal from yourself; if you strike another, you strike yourself; if you kill another, you kill yourself." This is the Right of RETALIATION (*jus talionis*); and properly understood, it is the only principle which in regulating a public court, as distinguished from mere private judgment, can definitely assign both the quality and the quantity of a just penalty. All other standards are wavering and uncertain; and on account of other considerations involved in them, they contain no principle conformable to the sentence of pure and strict justice.[2]

Obviously we could mull over this passage for a long time. What, exactly, is the distinction between the Inborn and the Civil Personality? How is the Penal Law a Categorical Imperative: by derivation from one of the five formulations in the *Grundlegung*, or as a separate formulation? But we are on the trail of the traditional retributive theory of punishment and do not want to lose ourselves in niceties. There are two main points in this passage to which we should give particular attention:

   i. The only acceptable reason for punishing a man is that he has commited a crime.

  ii. The only acceptable reason for punishing a man in a given manner and degree is that the punishment is "equal" to the crime for which he is punished.

These propositions, I think it will be agreed, express the main points of the first and second paragraphs respectively. Before stopping over these points, let us go on to a third. It is brought out in the following passage from the *Rechtslehre*, which is also often referred to by writers on retributivism.

> Even if a civil society resolved to dissolve itself with the consent of all its members—as might be supposed in the case of a people inhabiting an island resolving to separate and scatter themselves throughout the whole world—the last murderer lying in prison ought to be executed before the resolution was carried out. This ought to be done in order that every one may realize the desert of his deeds, and that bloodguiltiness may not remain upon the people; for otherwise they will all be regarded as participators in the murder as a public violation of justice.[3]

It is apparent from this passage that, so far anyway as the punishment of death for murder is concerned, the punishment awarded not only may but must be carried out. If it must be carried out "so that everyone may realize the desert of his deeds," then punishment for deeds other than murder must be carried out too. We will take it, then, that Kant holds that:

  iii. Whoever commits a crime must be punished in accordance with his desert.

Whereas (i) tells us what kind of reason we must have *if* we punish, (iii) now tells us that we must punish *whenever* there is desert of punishment. Punishment, Kant tells us elsewhere, is "The *juridical* effect or consequence of a culpable act of Demerit."[4] Any crime is a culpable act of demerit, in that it is an "*intentional* transgression—that is, an act accompanied with the consciousness that it is a transgression."[5] This is an unusually narrow definition of crime, since crime is not ordinarily limited to intentional acts of transgression, but may also include unintentional ones, such as acts done in ignorance of the law, and criminally negligent acts. However, Kant apparently leaves room for "culpable acts of demerit" outside of the category of crime. These he calls "faults," which are unintentional transgressions of duty, but "are nevertheless imputable to a person."[6] I can only suppose, though it is a difficulty in the interpretation of the *Rechtslehre*, that when Kant says that punishment must be inflicted "only because he has committed a crime," he is not including in "crime" what he would call a fault. Crime would, then, refer to any *intentional* imputable transgressions of duty; and these are what must be punished as involving ill desert. The difficulties involved in the definition of crime as the transgression of duty, as opposed to the mere violation of a legal prohibition, will be taken up later.

Taking the three propositions we have isolated as expressing the essence of the Kantian retributivistic position, we must now ask a direct and obvious question. What makes Kant hold this position? Why does he think it apparent that consequences should have *nothing to do* with the decision whether, and how, and how much to punish? There are two directions an answer to this question might follow. One would lead us into an extensive excursus on the philosophical position of Kant, the relation of this to his ethical theory, and the relation of his general theory of ethics to his philosophy of law. It would, in short, take our question as one about the consistency of Kant's position concerning the justification of punishment with the whole of the Kantian philosophy. This would involve discussion of Kant's reasons for believing that moral laws must be universal and categorical in virtue of their form alone, and divorced from any empirical content; of his attempt to make out a moral decision-procedure based upon an "empty" categorical imperative; and, above all, of the concept of freedom as a postulate of practical reason, and as the central concept of the philosophy of law. This kind of answer, however, we must forego here; for while it would have considerable interest in its own right, it would lead us astray from our purpose, which is to understand as well as we can the retributivist position, not as a part of this or that philosophical system but for its own sake. It is a position taken by philosophers with diverse philosophical systems; we want to take another direction, then, in our answer. Is there any *general*

(nonspecial, nonsystematic) reason why Kant rejects consequences in the justification of punishment?

Kant believes that consequences have nothing to do with the
justification of punishment partly because of his assumptions
about the *direction* of justification; and these assumptions are, I
believe, also to be found underlying the thought of Hegel and
Bradley. Justification is not only *of* something, it is also *to* someone: it has an addressee. Now there are important confusions in
Kant's and other traditional justifications of punishment turning
on the question what the "punishment" *is* which is being justified. In Chapter IV, we will examine some of these. But if we are
to feel the force of the retributivist position, we can no longer
put off the question of the addressee of justification.

To whom is the Kantian justification of punishment directed?
The question may seem a difficult one to answer, since Kant does
not consider it himself as a separate issue. Indeed, it is not the
kind of question likely to occur to a philosopher of Kant's formal-
istic leanings. A Kantian justification or rationale stands, so to
speak, on its own. It is a structure which can be examined, tested,
probed by any rational being. Even to speak of the addressee of
justification has an uncomfortably relativistic sound, as if only
persuasion of A or B or C is possible, and proof impossible. Yet,
in practice, Kant does not address his proffered justification of
punishment so much to any rational being (which, to put it
otherwise, is to address it not at all), as to the being most affect-
ed: the criminal himself.

It is the criminal who is cautioned not to creep through the
serpent-windings of utilitarianism. It is the criminal's rights
which are in question in the debate with Beccaria over capital
punishment. It is the criminal we are warned not to mix up with
property or things: the "subjects of Real Right." In the *Kritik
der Praktischen Vernunst,* the intended direction of justification
becomes especially clear.

> Now the notion of punishment, as such, cannot be united
> with that of becoming a partaker of happiness; for although
> he who inflicts the punishment may at the same time have the
> benevolent purpose of directing this punishment to this end,
> yet it must be justified in itself as punishment, i.e., as mere
> harm, so that if it stopped there, and the person punished could
> get no glimpse of kindness hidden behind this harshness, he

must yet admit that justice was done him, and that his reward was perfectly suitable to his conduct. In every punishment, as such, there must first be justice, and this constitutes the essence of the notion. Benevolence may, indeed, be united with it, but the man who has deserved punishment has not the least reason to reckon upon this.[7]

Since this matter of the direction of justification is central in our understanding of traditional retributivism, and not generally appreciated, it will be worth our while to pause over this paragraph. Kant holds here, as he later holds in the *Rechtslehre,* that once it has been decided that a given "mode and measure" of punishment is justified, then "he who inflicts punishment" may do so in such a way as to increase the long-term happiness of the criminal. This could be accomplished, e.g., by using a prison term as an opportunity for reforming the criminal. But Kant's point is that reforming the criminal has nothing to do with justifying the infliction of punishment. It is not inflicted because it will give an opportunity for reform, but because it is merited. The passage does not need my gloss; it is transparently clear. Kant wants the justification of punishment to be such that the criminal "who could get no glimpse of kindness behind this harshness" would have to admit that punishment is warranted.

Suppose we tell the criminal, "We are punishing you for your own good." This is wrong, because it is then open to him to raise the question whether he deserves punishment, and what you consider good to be. If he does not deserve punishment, we have no right to inflict it, especially in the name of some good of which the criminal may not approve. So long as we are to treat him as rational—a being with dignity—we cannot force our judgments of good upon him. This is what makes the appeal to supposedly good consequences "wavering and uncertain." They waver because the criminal has as much right as anyone to question them. They concern ends which he may reject, and means which he might rightly regard as unsuited to the ends .

In the "Supplementary Explanations of the Principles of Right" of the *Rechtslehre,* Kant distinguishes between "punitive justice (*justitia punitiva*), in which the ground of the penalty is moral (*quia peccatum est*)," and "punitive *expediency,* the foundation of which is merely pragmatic (*ne peccetur*) as being grounded upon the experience of what operates most effectively to prevent crime." Punitive justice, says Kant, has an "entirely distinct place (*locus justi*) in the topical arrangement of the juridical conceptions." It does not seem reasonable to suppose that Kant makes this distinction merely to discard punitive expediency entirely, that he has no concern at all for the *ne peccetur*. But he does hold that there is no place for it in the justification of punishment proper: for this can only be to show the criminal that the punishment is just.

How is this to be done? The difficulty is that on the one hand the criminal must be treated as a rational being, an end in himself; but on the other hand the justification we offer him cannot be allowed to appear as the opening move in a rational discussion. It cannot turn on the criminal's acceptance of some premise which, as rational being, he has a perfect right to question. If the end in question is the well-being of society, we are assuming that the criminal will not have a different view of what that well-being consists in, and we are telling him that he should sacrifice himself *to* that end. As a rational being, he can question whether any end we propose is a good end. And we have no right to demand that he sacrifice himself to the public well-being, even supposing he agrees with us on what that consists in. No man has a duty, on Kant's view, to be benevolent.[8]

The way out of the quandary is to show the criminal that we are not inflicting the punishment on him for some questionable purpose of our own choice, but that he, as a free agent, has exercised *his* choice in such a way as to make the punishment a necessary consequence. "His own evil deed draws the punishment upon himself."[9] "The undeserved evil which anyone commits on another, is to tbe regarded as perpetuated on himself."[10] But may not the criminal rationally question this asserted connection between crime and punishment? Suppose he wishes to regard the punishment *not* as "drawn upon himself" by his own "evil deed?" Suppose he argues that no good purpose will be served by punishing him? But this line of thought leads into the "serpent-windings of utilitarianism," for if it is good consequences that govern, then justice goes by the board. What may not be done to him in the name of good consequences? What proportion would remain between what he has done and what he suffers?[11]

But punishment is *inflicted*. To tell the criminal that he "draws it upon himself" is all very well, only how do we justify *to ourselves* the infliction of it? Kant's answer is found early in the *Rechtslehre*.[12] There he relates punishment to crime *via* freedom. Crime consists in compulsion or constraint of some kind: a hindrance of freedom.[13] If it is wrong that freedom should be hindered, it is right to block this hindrance. But to block the constraint of freedom it is necessary to apply constraint. Punishment is a"hindering of a hindrance of freedom." Compulsion of the criminal is, then, justified only to the extent that it hinders his compulsion of another.

But how are we to understand Kant here? Punishment comes after the crime. How can it hinder the crime? The reference cannot be to the hindrance of future crime, or Kant's doctrine reduces to a variety of utilitarianism. The picture of compulsion *vs.* compulsion is clear enough, but how are we to apply it? Our answer must be somewhat speculative, since there is no direct answer to be found in the *Rechtslehre*. The answer must begin from yet another extension of the concept of a crime. For the crime cannot consist merely in an act. What is criminal is acting in accordance with a wrong maxim: a maxim which would, if made universal, destroy freedom. The adoption of the maxim is criminal. Should we regard punishment, then, as the hindrance of a wrong maxim? But how do we hinder a maxim? We show, exhibit, its wrongness by taking it at face value. If the criminal has adopted it, he is claiming that it can be universalized. But if it is universalized it warrants the same treatment of the criminal as he has accorded to his victim. So if he murders he must be executed; if he steals we must "steal from" him.[14] What we do to him he willed, in willing to adopt his maxim as universalizable. To justify the punishment to the criminal is to show him that the compulsion we use on him proceeds according to the same rule by which he acts. This is how he "draws the punishment upon himself." In punishing, we are not adopting his maxim but demonstrating its logical consequences if universalized: we show the criminal *what* he has willed. This is the positive side of the Kantian rationale of punishment.

II

Hegel's version of this rationale has attracted more attention, and disagreement, in recent literature. It is the Hegelian metaphysical terminology which is in part responsible for the disagreement, and which has stood in the way of an understanding of the retributivist position. The difficulty turns around the notions of "annulment of crime," and of punishment as the "right" of the criminal. Let us consider "annulment" first.

In the *Philosophie des Rechts*[15] Hegel tells us that

> Abstract right is a right to coerce, because the wrong which transgresses it is an exercise of force against the existence of my freedom in an external thing. The maintenance of this existent against the exercise of force therefore itself takes the form of an external act and an exercise of force annulling the force originally brought against it.[16]

Holmes complains that by the use of his logical apparatus, involving the negation of negations (or annulment), Hegel professes to establish what is only a mystic (though generally felt) bond between wrong and punishment.[17] Hastings Rashdall asks how any rational connection can be shown between the evil of the pain of punishment, and the twin evils of the suffering of the victim and the moral evil which "pollutes the offender's soul," unless appeal is made to the probable good consequences of punishment. The notion that the "guilt" of the offense must be, in some mysterious way, wiped out by the suffering of the offender does not seem to provide it.[18] Crime, which is an evil, is apparently to be "annulled" by the addition to it of punishment, which is another evil. How can two evils yield a good?[19]

But in fact Hegel is following the *Rechtslehre* quite closely here, and his doctrine is very near to Kant's. In the notes taken at Hegel's lectures,[20] we find Hegel quoted as follows:

> If crime and its annulment . . . are treated as if they were unqualified evils, it must, of course, seem quite unreasonable to will an evil merely because "another evil is there already." . . . But it is not merely a question of an evil or of this, that, or the other good; the precise point at issue is wrong, and the righting of it. . . . The various considerations which are relevant to punishment as a phenomenon and to the bearing it has on the particular consciousness, and which concern its effects (deterrent, reformative, etc.) on the imagination, are an essential topic for examination in their place, especially in connection with modes of punishment, but all these considerations presuppose as their foundation the fact that punishment is inherently and actually just. In discussing this matter the only

important things are, first, that crime is to be annulled, not because it is the producing of an evil, but because it is the infringing of the right as right, and secondly, the question of what that positive existence is which crime possesses and which must be annulled; it is this existence which is the real evil to be removed, and the essential point is the question of where it lies. So long as the concepts here at issue are not clearly apprehended, confusion must continue to reign in the theory of punishment.[21]

While this passage is not likely to dethrone confusion, it does bring us closer to the basically Kantian heart of Hegel's theory. To "annul crime" should be read "right wrong." Crime is a wrong which consists in an "infringement of the right as right."[22] It would be unjust, says Hegel, to allow crime, which is the invasion of a right, to go unrequited. For to allow this is to admit that the crime is "valid": that is, that it is not in conflict with justice. But this is what we do want to admit, and the only way of showing this is to pay back the deed to the agent: coerce the coercer. For by intentionally violating his victim's rights, the criminal in effect claims that the rights of others are not binding on him; and this is to attack *das Recht* itself: the system of justice in which there are rights which must be respected. Punishment not only keeps the system in balance, it vindicates the system itself.

Besides talking about punishment's "annulment" of crime, Hegel has argued that it is the "right of the criminal." The obvious reaction to this is that it is a strange justification of punishment which makes it someone's right, for it is at best a strange kind of right which no one would ever want to claim! McTaggart's explanation of this facet of Hegel's theory is epitomized in the following quotation:

What, then, is Hegel's theory? It is, I think, briefly this: In sin, man rejects and defies the moral law. Punishment is pain inflicted on him because he has done this, and in order that he may, by the fact of his punishment, be forced into recognizing as valid the law which he rejected in sinning, and so repent of his sin—really repent, and not merely be frightened out of doing it again.[23]

If McTaggart is right, then we are obviously not going to find in Hegel anything relevant to the justification of legal punishment, where the notions of sin and repentance are out of place.

And this is the conclusion McTaggart of course reaches. "Hegel's view of punishment," he insists, "cannot properly be applied in jurisprudence, and . . . his chief mistake regarding it lay in supposing that it could."[24]

But though McTaggart may be right in emphasizing the theological aspect of Hegel's doctrine of punishment, he is wrong in denying it a jurisprudential aspect. In fact, Hegel is only saying what Kant emphasized: that to justify punishment to the criminal is to show him that *he* has chosen to be treated as he is being treated.

> The injury (the penalty) which falls on the criminal is not merely *implicitly* just—as just, it is *eo ipso* his implicit will, an embodiment of his freedom, his right; on the contrary, it is also a right *established* within the criminal himself, i.e. in his objectively embodied will, in his action. The reason for this is that his action is the action of a rational being and this implies that it is something universal and that by doing it the criminal has laid down a law which he has explicitly recognized in his action and under which in consequence he should be brought as under his right.[25]

To accept the retributivist position, then, is to accept a thesis about the burden of proof in the justification of punishment. Provided we make the punishment "equal" to the crime it is not up to us to justify it to the criminal, beyond pointing out to him that it is what he willed. It is not that he initiated a chain of events likely to result in his punishment, but that in willing the crime he willed that he himself should suffer in the same degree as his victim. But what if the criminal simply wanted to commit his crime and get away with it (break the window and run, take the funds and retire to Brazil, kill but live?) Suppose we explain to the criminal that *really* in willing to kill he willed to lose his life; and, unimpressed, he replies that *really* he wished to kill and save his skin. The retributivist answer is that to the extent that the criminal understands freedom and justice he will understand that his punishment was made inevitable by his own choice. No moral theory can hope to provide a justification of punishment which will seem such to the criminal merely as a nexus of passions and desires. The retributivist addresses him as a rational being, aware of the significance of his action. The burden of proof, the retributivist would argue, is on the theorist who would not start from this assumption. For to assume from the beginning that the criminal is not rational is to treat him, from the beginning, as merely a "harmful animal."

> What is involved in the action of the criminal is not only the concept of crime, the rational aspect present in crime as such whether the individual wills it or not, the aspect which the state has to vindicate, but also the abstract rationality of the individual's *volition*. Since that is so, punishment is regarded as containing the criminal's right and hence by being punished he is honored as a rational being. He does not receive this due of honor unless the concept and measure of his punishment are derived from his own act. Still less does he receive it if he is treated as a harmful animal who has to be made harmless, or with a view to deterring and reforming him.[26]

To address the criminal as a rational being aware of the significance of his action is to address him as a person who knows that he has not committed a "bare" act; to commit an act is to commit oneself to the universalization of the rule by which one acted. For a man to complain about the death sentence for murder is as absurd as for a man to complain that when he pushes down one tray of the scales, the other tray goes up; whereas the action, rightly considered, is of pushing down *and* up. "The criminal gives his consent already by his very act."[27] "The Eumenides sleep, but crime awakens them, and hence it is the very act of crime which vindicates itself."[28]

F. H. Bradley's contribution to the retributive theory of punishment adds heat but not much light. The central, and best-known, passage is the following:

> If there is any opinion to which the man of uncultivated morals is attached, it is the belief in the necessary connection of Punishment and guilt. Punishment is punishment, only where it is deserved. We pay the penalty because we owe it, and for no other reason; and if punishment is inflicted for any other reason whatever than because it is merited by wrong, it is a gross immorality, a crying injustice, an abominable crime, and not what it pretends to be. We may have regard for whatever considerations we please—our own convenience, the good of society, the benefit of the offender; we are fools, and worse, if we fail to do so. Having once the right to punish, we may modify the punishment according to the useful and the pleasant; but

these are external to the matter, they cannot give us a right to punish, and nothing can do that but criminal desert. This is not a subject to waste words over; if the fact of the vulgar view is not palpable to the reader, we have no hope, and no wish, to make it so.[29]

Bradley's sympathy with the "vulgar view" should be apparent.[30] And there is at least a seeming variation between the position he expresses here and that we have attributed to Kant and Hegel. For Bradley can be read here as leaving an open field for utilitarian reasoning, when the question is how and how much to punish. Ewing interprets Bradley this way, and argues at some length that Bradley is involved in an inconsistency.[31] However, it is quite possible that Bradley did not mean to allow kind and quantity of punishment to be determined by utilitarian considerations. He could mean, as Kant meant, that once punishment is awarded, then "it" (what the criminal must suffer: time in jail, e.g.) may be made use of for utilitarian purposes. But, it should by this time go without saying, the retributivist would then wish to insist that we not argue backward from the likelihood of attaining these good purposes to the rightness of inflicting the punishment.

Bradley's language is beyond question loose when he speaks, in the passage quoted, of our "modifying" the punishment, "having once the right to punish." But when he says that "we pay the penalty because we owe it, and for no other reason," Bradley must surely be credited with the insight that we may owe more or less according to the gravity of the crime. The popular view, he says, is "that punishment is justice; that justice implies the giving what is due."[32] And, "punishment is the complement of criminal desert; is justifiable only so far as deserved."[33] If Bradley accepts this popular view, then Ewing must be wrong in attributing to him the position that kind and degree of punishment may be determined by utilitarian considerations.[34]

III

Let us sum up traditional retributivism, as we have found it expressed in the paradigmatic passage we have examined. We have found no reason, in Hegel or Bradley, to take back or qualify importantly the *three propositions* we found central in Kant's retributivism:

i. The only acceptable reason for punishing a man is that he has committed a crime.

ii. The only acceptable reason for punishing a man in a given manner and degree is that the punishment is "equal' 'to the crime.

iii. Whoever commits a crime must be punished in accordance with his desert.

To these propositions should be added *two underlying assumptions:*

i. An assumption about the direction of justification: to the criminal.

ii. An assumption about the nature of justification: to show the criminal that it is he who has willed what he now suffers.

Though it may have been stated in forbidding metaphysical terms, traditional retributivism cannot be dismissed as unintelligible, or absurd, or implausible.[35] There is no obvious contradiction in it; and there are no important disagreements between the philosophers we have studied over what it contends. Yet in spite of the importance of the theory, no one has yet done much more than sketch it in broad strokes. If, as I have surmised, it turns mainly on an assumption concerning the direction of justification, then this assumption should be explained and defended.

And the key concept of "desert" is intolerably vague. What does it mean to say that punishment must be proportionate to what a man *deserves?* This seems to imply, in the theory of the traditional retributivists, that there is some way of measuring desert, or at least of balancing punishment against it. How this measuring or balancing is supposed to be done, we will discuss later. What we must recognize here is that there are alternative criteria of "desert," and that it is not always clear which of these the traditional retributivist means to imply.

When we say of a man that he "deserves severe punishment" how, if at all, may we support our position by arguments? What kinds of considerations tend to show what a man does or does not deserve? There are at least two general sorts: those which tend to show that what he has done is a member of a class of actions which is especially heinous; and those which tend to show that his doing of this action was, in (or because of) the circumstances, particularly wicked. The argument that a man deserves punishment may rest on the first kind of appeal alone, or on both kinds. Retributivists who rely on the first sort of consideration alone would say that anyone who would do a certain sort of thing, no matter what the circumstances may have been, deserves punishment. Whether there are any such retributivists I do not know. Kant, because of his insistence on *intention* as a necessary condition of committing a crime, clearly wishes to bring in considerations of the second sort as well. It is not, on his view, merely *what* was done, but the intention of the agent which must be taken into account. No matter what the intention, a man cannot commit a crime deserving punishment if his deed is not a transgression. But if he does commit a transgression, he must do so intentionally to commit a crime; and all crime is deserving of punishment. The desert of the crime is a factor both of the seriousness of the transgression, considered by itself, and the degree to which the intention to transgress was present. If, for Kant, the essence of morality consists in knowingly acting from duty, the essence of immorality consists in knowingly acting against duty.

The retributivist can perhaps avoid the question of how we decide that one crime is morally more heinous than another by hewing to his position that no such decision is necessary so long as we make the punishment "equal" to the crime. To accomplish this, he might argue, it is not necessary to argue to the *relative* wickedness of crimes. But at best this leaves us with the problem how we *do* make punishments equal to crimes, a problem which will not stop plaguing retributivists. And there is the problem *which* transgressions, intentionally committed, the retributivist is to regard as crimes. Surely not every morally wrong action![36]

And how is the retributivist to fit in appeals to punitive expediency? None of our authors deny that such appeals may be made, but where and how do they tie into punitive justice? It will not do simply to say that justifying punishment to the criminal is one thing, and justifying it to society is another. Suppose we must justify in both directions at once? And who are "we" anyway— the players of which roles, at what stage of the game?[37] And has the retributivist cleared himself of the charge, sure to arise, that the theory is but a cover for a much less commendable motive than respect for justice: elegant draping for naked revenge?[38]

IV

The utilitarian theory of punishment can be regarded as but a subheading of a highly developed general theory of ethics which has had numerous advocates in the history of philosophy, and remains popular today. It is therefore tempting to begin our analysis with some very general formulation of utilitarianism (e.g. "An act, policy, course of action, or practice is right if and only if the set of consequences it initiates would be better on the whole than the consequences initiated by any alternative act, policy, course of action, or practice.") and to show how, if this general position be accepted, the special utilitarian theory of punishment follows. But this approach would be mistaken. It would lead us to settle by fiat a vigorous debate among utilitarians over the way in which the general position should be formulated and defended. (Should acts be justified by reference to rules, rules by reference to practices, and practices by reference to their tendency to maximize good consequences; or should we reserve the right to short-cut the rules and practices, and calculate the consequences of the act? And what are the consequences which should be maximized?) It would also lead us to ignore the real possibility that a philosopher might without inconsistency adopt a utilitarian position with respect to punishment, but reject it as a general theory of ethics.

Our concern must be, rather, at this stage of our analysis, to delineate as sharply as possible the general outlines of the traditional utilitarian theory of punishment: to set it out, if we can, in propositions which can be contrasted with those we have taken as expressing the retributive position. To accomplish this we turn again to the history of philosophy, to philosophers generally accepted as promulgating a utilitarian view of punishment. Here, as in the previous section, we will make no attempt to survey the whole field, but will discuss positions which would be universally accepted as paradigmatic: those of William Paley and Jeremy Bentham.

There are advantages in beginning with William Paley beyond that of mere chronological appropriateness. Paley's formulation of the utilitarian theory of punishment was enormously influential, since it was expressed in a book which was a text at Cambridge, and a standard reference on philosophy, running through fifteen

editions in Paley's own lifetime.[39] So highly regarded was this
book, and so conservative in tendency, that Sir Samuel Romilly,
the great reformer of the English criminal law, was obliged to
devote a large proportion of his major address of 1810 to a critical
analysis of it.[40] More importantly for our purposes, it provides
us with a bold and uncomplicated first statement of the position
we wish to understand.

"The proper end of human punishment is not," Paley tells us,
"the satisfaction of justice, but the prevention of crimes." And
since the prevention of crimes is the "sole consideration which
authorizes the infliction of punishment by human laws," punishment must be proportioned to prevention, not to guilt. "The crime
must be prevented by some means or other; and consequently,
whatever means appear necessary to this end, whether they be
proportionable to the guilt of the criminal or not, are adopted
rightly, because they are adopted upon the principle which alone
justifies the infliction of punishment at all." Since punishment is
itself an evil, it should be resorted to only when a greater evil
can be prevented. "The sanguinary laws which have been made
against counterfeiting or diminishing the gold coin of the king-
dom might be just, until the method of detecting the fraud by
weighing the money, was introduced into general usage." The
facility with which a crime can be committed constitutes a ground
for more severe punishment. The stealing of cloth from bleaching
grounds must be punished more severely than most other simple
felonies not because this crime is in its "own nature more heinous"
but because the property is more exposed.[41]

"From the justice of God," says Paley, "we are taught to look
for a graduation of punishment, exactly proportioned to the guilt
of the offender." But, not finding this proportion in human law,
we question its wisdom. However, we must recognize that

> when the care of the public safety is entrusted to men, whose
> authority over their fellow creatures is limited by defects of
> power and knowledge; from whose utmost vigilance and sagac-
> ity the greatest offenders often lie hid; whose wisest precau-
> tions and speediest pursuit may be eluded by artifice or con-
> cealment; a different necessity, a new rule of proceeding results
> from the very imperfection of their faculties. In their hands the
> uncertainty of punishment must be compensated by the severity.
> The ease with which crimes are committed or concealed, must

be counteracted by additional penalities and increased terrors. The very end for which human government is established, requires that its regulations be adapted to the suppression of crimes. This end, whatever it may do in the plans of infinite wisdom, does not in the designation of temporal penalties, always coincide with the proportionate punishment of guilt.[42]

This is flat opposition to retributivism. To Kant's thesis that the only reason for which we may punish is that a crime has been committed, Paley replies that the only reason for punishment is the prevention of crime. To Kant's thesis that the only ground for choosing a given "mode and measure" of punishment is that it equals the crime, Paley counters that mode and measure must be determined by the utility of the proposed punishment in preventing crime. Paley could not agree that the last prisoner, in Kant's example of the dispersing community, should be executed; since he holds that if crime can be prevented by means short of punishment it should be, but it is a truism that if the community is dispersed the opportunity for crime will not arise again in the community. To each of the propositions to which we reduced Kantian retributivism, Paley would oppose a contrary proposition.

i. The only acceptable reason for punishing a man is that punishing him will serve the end of the prevention of crimes.

ii. The only acceptable reason for punishing a man in a given manner and degree is that this is the manner and degree of punishment most likely to prevent the crime.

iii. Whether or not a man should be punished depends upon the possibility of preventing the crime in question by non-punitive means.

V

Paley's theory of punishment is but a sketch, so cryptic that we do not know what directions he might have taken in developing it. Bentham's is the most comprehensive theory in the history of philosophy.[43] He extends Paley's theory by: (1) Providing a general theoretical foundation for the justification of punishment; (2) Distinguishing carefully between punishment and other "remedies" for crime; (3) Drawing the limits beyond which punishment should not be applied; and (4) Offering rules for the determination of manner and degree of punishing.

In the wealth of important material to be found in Bentham's published work on the subject of punishment, any selection is bound to seem arbitrary; yet select we must. Our object will be merely to give some indication of what traditional utilitarianism with respect to punishment is like in its most highly developed form.

(1) *Theoretical foundation.* Bentham is not content to begin with the purpose of punishment, but, thinking of punishment as but one tool in the hands of the legislator, asks what the end is which this and other legislative tools should be made to serve. This end is "to augment the total happiness of the community; and therefore, in the first place, to exclude, as far as may be, every thing that tends to subtract from happiness: in other words to exclude mischief."[44]

This broader foundation will allow Bentham to include more under punishment than prevention of crimes as they arise, and to take a wider view of prevention than Paley did. Bentham agrees with Paley that punishment is itself an evil and should, if used, be used as sparingly as possible: "Upon the principle of utility, if it ought at all to be admitted, it ought only to be admitted in as far as it promises to exclude some greater evil." But here again he takes a wider view, by setting for himself the task of discriminating between those situations in which punishment should be used and those in which it should not.

(2) *Distinction between punishment and other possible remedies for crime.* The mischief of crime obstructs happiness, but the mischief of punishment does too; so we must be chary in our use of punishment and look about for other means of dealing with the mischief of crime. All such means, including punishment, Bentham terms "remedies," and there are four sorts: (a) Preventive, (b) Suppressive, (c) Satisfactory, and (d) Penal remedies or Punishment.

(a) The first of these remedies has an unfortunate title, since on Bentham's view, punishment is preventive also. What he has in mind are, first, direct moves which can be made by the police or private citizens, like admonitions, threats, or seizure of arms, to prevent the occurrences of a particular crime which is thought likely to occur: as when we see a man apparently preparing to commit armed robbery and warn him away.[45] Secondly, there is the whole vast class of indirect moves which can be made to prevent crime: indirect in that they refer not to this or that particular crime, but to a class of crimes which might be committed—preventive medicine as opposed to treating the cholera of crime when it breaks out. Under this important heading, Bentham discusses[46] at length such topics as removal of temptations to crime, like easily concealed arms and tools for the counterfeiting of money; substituting innocuous for dangerous desires and inclinations; and putting people on guard against certain types of offenses.

(b) Suppressive remedies "tend to put a stop to an offense in progress, but not completed, and so prevent the evil, or at least a part of it."[47] Bentham gives no examples, but mentions that suppressive means are the same as preventive ones. The difference apparently lies in the stage of the game at which they are applied: the crime of murder is suppressed if we wrest away the would-be killer's gun, prevented if we warn his victim to leave town or pass and enforce a law prohibiting the sale of weapons which can easily be concealed.

(c) Satisfactory remedies "consist of reparations or indemnities, secured to those who have suffered from offenses."[48] They assume the crime done and try to remove all or part of the mischief it caused. Thus the money taken from the bank must be returned, the damage to a house repaired, the public calumny publicly admitted to be false. The object is to make it as if the crime had never occurred. The object is not, as with Kant's Principle of Equality, that the criminal must suffer in the way and to the degree that his victim suffered; but that the suffering of the victim must somehow be compensated to him.[49]

(d) Punishment is distinguished from the other remedies for the mischief of crime in that, like satisfactory remedies, it occurs only after the crime, but, unlike satisfactory remedies, its purpose is preventive: "to prevent like offenses, whether on the part of the offender or of others."

What is past is but one act; the future is infinite. The offense already committed concerns only a single individual; similar offenses may affect all. In many cases it is impossible to redress the evil that is done; but it is always possible to take away the will to repeat it; for however great may be the advantage of the offense, the evil of the punishment may be always made out to outweigh it.[51]

The punishment which serves to deter the criminal from repeating his crime is called by Bentham "particular prevention." This may be achieved in three ways: by taking away from the criminal the physical power of repeating his offense (incapacitation), by taking away the desire of offending (reformation), or by making him afraid of offending (intimidation). It is general prevention, however, the prevention of crime by example of the punishment suffered by the offender, which "ought to be the chief end of punishment, as it is its real justification."[52]

> That punishment which, considered in itself, appeared base and repugnant to all generous sentiments, is elevated to the first rank of benefits, when it is regarded not as an act of wrath or of vengeance against a guilty or unfortunate individual who has given way to mischievous inclinations, but as an indispensable sacrifice to the common safety.[53]

(3) *The limits of punishment.* When we understand that punishment is but one of the remedies which may be used against crime, and the conditions under which and the purpose for which it should be used, we are ready to approach the topic of the limits of punishment: "cases unmeet for punishment." Given the general preventive end of punishment, it ought not to be inflicted where it is (a) groundless, (b) inefficacious, (c) unprofitable, or (d) needless. Since punishment is itself an evil, the burden of proof is on him who would inflict it, and this is so even though a crime has been committed. This contrasts with traditional retributivism, where the burden is on the criminal to show why he should not be punished equally with his crime, but does not rest (provided the proper proportion is observed) on the person inflicting punishment.

(a) Punishment is groundless when there is no mischief for it to prevent. For example, though it seemed mischievous (breaking into a man's house, burning his fields), yet the "victim" gave his (free and fairly obtained) consent; or though it is mischievous it was necessary as a means to an over-all good (tearing down a man's house to get material for plugging the dike).

(b) Punishment is inefficacious when it cannot act preventively. Examples are *ex-post facto* laws; laws not sufficiently promulgated; punishment of infants or insane persons, or persons under physical compulsion.

(c) Punishment is unprofitable when the punishment would produce more evil than the offense it is meant to prevent (capital punishment for picking pockets).

(d) Punishment is needless when the mischief can be prevented at a "cheaper rate." This limitation (recognized by Paley in the coinage example mentioned above) comes about when there is some means short of punishment which will accomplish the same thing. (Instructing misguided people concerning the moral principles by which they should be guided.)[54]

(4) *Rules for the determination of manner and degree of punishment.* It is here that the subtlety and caution of Bentham are especially apparent. He could not be satisfied with Paley's rough dictum that the crime must be prevented by some means or other and that proportion between guilt and punishment must therefore be ignored. Among the factors (to be examined in more detail later) which Bentham considers, are the need to set penalties in such a way that where a person is tempted to commit one of two crimes he will commit the lesser, that the evil consequences (mischief) of the crime will be minimized even if the crime is committed, that the least amount possible of punishment be used for the prevention of a given crime.

VI

That Bentham moves well beyond Paley in intelligibility and careful analysis there can be no question. Does the Benthamite analysis conflict with the Paleian position: force us to alter the formulation of the utilitarian theory of punishment which we understood Paley to express? It does not so much require alteration as careful qualification of the bare and bold Paleian pronouncements:

   i. The only acceptable reason for punishing a man is that punishing him will serve the end of the prevention of crimes.

Yes, Bentham would say, but we must not forget that there are some deeds it will not be worthwhile to denominate crimes and try to prevent; nor that prevention is itself a very complex notion, the analysis of which bears importantly on the means we use.

ii. The only acceptable reason for punishing a man in a given manner and degree is that this manner and degree of punishment is most likely to prevent the crime.

Bentham would add: Consistently with the reduction of mischief in general! We cannot look at the prevention of each crime as a separate problem. We want to reduce the mischief of *all* crime at the least possible expense. Otherwise, we will fall into feckless severity, as did Madan, and Paley himself.

iii. Whether or not a man should be punished depends upon the possibility of preventing the crime in question by nonpunitive means.

Yes, Bentham would agree, since punishment is but one of four possible remedies for crime, and should be reserved until remedies involving less mischief have been tried.

Paley looks only to the prevention of the crime in question, or (at best) of crimes in general. For Bentham, prevention of crime is but a subheading under prevention of mischief, and that a subheading under the promotion of happiness. But since there is no question but what mischief must be prevented if happiness is to be promoted, and that crime is mischief, the justification of punishment turns inevitably only on the prevention of crime at the least cost, in mischief, of the means used.

It is, of course, the word "only" which gives rise to the trouble, for the retributivist creed has an "only" in it, too: it is only by reference to desert that punishment may be justified. Both of these positions cannot be true, so much is obvious. And both could be false.

If we were to follow out the lead developed in the first section, we would look for the addressee, if there is just one, of the Benthamite justification of punishment. And we would find that Bentham does not appear to have so much in mind justification to the criminal (or to any of us who might have to play that role) as justification to the noninvolved citizen whose interest is simply in the best ordering of society. But to make this out in detail would be tedious. It might also be misleading, for it might suggest that the whole controversy could be resolved by showing that the retributivist is talking to one addressee and is concerned with one set of problems, and the utilitarian to another and another set of problems.

This is indeed a promising approach, for it looks as if it might be a way out of the ancient quandary. And it is not far from the road we shall now follow, which will lead us to distinguish a number of disparate undertakings which have traditionally been lumped together as "the justification of punishment." Whether these distinctions, once made, will resolve the quandary remains to be seen.

CHAPTER I

FOOTNOTES

1. What is the cause of this difficulty? Perhaps it is mainly that, since in our own time there are few defenders of retributivism, the position is most often referred to by writers who are opposed to it. This does not make for clarity. In the past few years, however, there has been an upsurge of interest, and some good articles have been written. Cf. esp. J. D. Mabbott, "Punishment," *Mind,* XLVIII (1939), pp. 152-67; C. S. Lewis, "The Humanitarian Theory of Punishment," *20th Century* (Australian), March, 1949; C. W. K. Mundle, "Punishment and Desert," *The Philosophical Quarterly,* IV (1954), pp. 216-228; A. S. Kaufman, "Anthony Quinton on Punishment," *Analysis,* October, 1959; and K. G. Armstrong, "The Retributivist Hits Back," LXX (1961), pp. 471-90.
2. *Rechtslehre,* Part Second, 49, E. Hastie translation, Edinburgh, 1887, pp. 195-7.
3. *Ibid.,* p. 198. Cf. also the passage on p. 196 beginning "What, then, is to be said of such a proposal as to keep a Criminal alive who has been condemned to death . . ."
4. *Ibid.,* Prolegomena, General Divisions of the Metaphysic of Morals, IV. (Hastie, p. 38).
5. *Ibid.,* p. 32.
6. *Ibid.,* p. 32.
7. Book I, Ch. I, Sect. VIII, Theorem IV, Remark II (T. K. Abbott translation, 5th ed., revised, London, 1898, p. 127).
8. *Rechtslehre.*
9. "Supplementary Explanation of The Principles of Right," V.
10. Cf. long quote from the *Rechtslehre,* above.
11. How can the retributivist allow utilitarian considerations even in the administration of the sentence? Are we not then opportunistically imposing our conception of good on the convicted man? How did we come by this right, which we did not have when he stood before the bar awaiting sentence? Kant would refer to the loss of his "Civil Personality;" but what rights remain with the "Inborn Personality," which is not lost? How is human dignity modified by conviction of crime?
12. Introduction to The Science of Right, General Definitions and Divisions, D. Right is Joined with the Title to Compel. (Hastie, p. 47).
13. This extends the definition of crime Kant has given earlier by specifying the nature of an imputable transgression of duty.
14. There are serious difficulties in the application of the "Principle of Equality"

to the "mode and measure" of punishment. This will be considered in Chapter V.

15. I shall use this short title for the work with the formidable double title of *Naturrecht und Staatswissenchaft in Grundrisse; Grundlinien der Philosophie des Rechts (Natural Law and Poitical Science in Outline; Elements of The Philosophy of Right.)* References will be to the T. M. Knox translation (*Hegel's Philosophy of Right*, Oxford, 1942).

16. *Philosophie des Rechts*, Sect. 93 (Knox, p. 67).

17. O. W. Holmes, Jr., *The Common Law*, Boston, 1881, p. 42.

18. Hastings Rashdall, *The Theory of Good and Evil*, 2nd. Edn., Oxford, 1924, vol. 1, pp. 285-6.

19. G. E. Moore holds that, consistently with his doctrine of organic wholes, they might; or at least they might yield that which is less evil than the sum of the constituent evils. This indicates for him a possible vindication of the Retributive theory of punishment. (*Principia Ethica*, Cambridge, 1903, pp. 213-214).

20. Included in the Knox translation.

21. Knox translation, pp. 69-70.

22. There is an unfortunate ambiguity in the German word *Recht,* here translated as "right." The word can mean either that which is a right or that which is in accordance with the law. So when Hegel speaks of "infringing the right as right" it is not certain whether he means a right as such or the law as such, or whether, in fact, he is aware of the ambiguity. But to say that the crime infringes the law is analytic, so we will take it that Hegel uses *Recht* here to refer to that which is right. But what the criminal does is not merely to infringe a right, but "the right (*das Recht*) as right," that is, to challenge by his action the whole system of rights. (On "*Recht,*" Cf. J. Austin, *The Province of Jurisprudence Determined*, London, Library of Ideas end., 1954), Note 26, pp. 285-288 esp. pp. 287-8).

23. J. M. E. McTaggart, *Studies in The Hegelian Cosmology,* Cambridge, 1901, Ch. V, p. 133.

24. *Ibid.,* p. 145.

25. *Op. Cit.,* Sect. 100 (Hastie, p. 70.)

26. *Ibid.,* Lecture-notes on Sect. 100, Hastie, p. 71.

27. *Ibid.,* Addition to Sect. 100, Hastie, p. 246.

28. *Ibid.,* Addition to Sect. 101, Hastie, p. 247. There is something ineradicably *curious* about retributivism. We keep coming back to the metaphor of the balance scale. Why is the metaphor powerful and the same time strange? Why do we agree so readily that "the assassination" cannot "trammel up the consequence," that "even-handed justice comments th' ingredients of our poisoned chalice to our own lips?"

29. F. H. Bradley, *Ethical Studies,* Oxford, 1952, pp. 26-7. Bradley's later article, "Some Remarks on Punishment" is considered in Chapter V.

30. Yet it may not be amiss to note the part played by the "vulgar view" in Bradley's essay. In "The Vulgar Notion of Responsibility in Connection with the Theories of Free Will and Necessity," from which this passage is quoted, Bradley is concerned to show that neither the "Libertarian" nor the "Necessitarian" position can be accepted. Both of these "two great schools" which "divide our philosophy" "stand out of relation to vulgar morality." Bradley suggests that perhaps the truth is to be found not in either of these "two undying and opposite one-sidednesses but in a philosophy which "thinks what the vulgar believe." Cf. also the contrasting of the "ordinary consciousness" with the "philosophical" or "debauched" morality (p. 4). On p. 3 he says that by going to "vulgar morality" we "gain in integrity" what we "lose in refinement." Nevertheless, he does say (p. 4) "seeing the vulgar are after all the vulgar, we should not be at pains to agree with their superstitions."

31. A. C. Ewing, *The Morality of Punishment,* London, 1929, pp. 41-42.

32. *Op. Cit.,* p. 29.

33. *Ibid.,* p. 30.
34. *Op. Cit.,* p. 41.
35. Or, more ingeniously, "merely logical," the "elucidation of the use of a word;" answering the question, "When (logically) *can* we punish?" as opposed to the question answered by the utilitarians, "When (morally) *may* or *ought* we to punish?" (Cf. A. M. Quinton, "On Punishment," *Analysis,* June, 1954, pp. 133-142).
36. Cf. Ch. V.
37. Distinctions to be made in Chapter III.
38. To be discussed in the next chapter.
39. *The Principles of Moral and Political Philosophy.* References are to the 6th edition, corrected, London, 1788.
40. L. Radzinowicz, *A History of English Criminal Law and its Administration from 1750.* London, 1948, pp. 257-259.
41. *Op. Cit.,* Vol. II, Book VI, Ch. IX, pp. 268-70.
42. *Ibid.,* pp. 273-4.
43. The sources used here are *Introduction to the Principles of Morals and Legislation,* Wilfrid Harrison, ed., Oxford, 1948; *The Theory of Legislation,* originally edited and published in French by Etienne Dumont re-translated, and re-edited by C. K. Ogden, London, 1931; and *The Rationale of Punishment,* also re-translated from Dumont's edition, London, 1830. There is much overlap in these books, which were all mined from the same lode of manuscripts. Where there is overlap, reference will be made to the *Principles* or the *Theory,* since the *Rationale* is out of print and not generally available.
44. *Principles,* p. 281.
45. Examples are mainly mine, here and in the following paragraphs, since Bentham gives few.
46. *Theory,* "Principles of The Penal Code," IV (pp. 358-472).
47. *Ibid.,* p. 271.
48. *Ibid.,* p. 271.
49. A connecting link could be the vindictive satisfaction felt by the victim on seeing the criminal punished, considered as compensation to the victim. But the victim may not want this kind of "compensation." (Cf. *Theory,* Principles of the Penal Code, II, XVI).
50. *Ibid.,* p. 272.
51. *Ibid.,* p. 272.
52. *Rationale,* I, III, p. 20.
53. *Ibid.,* p. 21.
54. *Priniples,* pp. 281-288.

THE IMPASSE

One cause is good until the other's understood.

Poor Robin's Almanac

Traditional retributivists hold that it is only by reference to what a man deserves for his crime that punishment can be justified (at all, and in a given manner and degree); traditional utilitarians hold that punishment can be justified only by reference to prevention of crime. The positions are, on the face of it, contraries. Both cannot be true, though both could be false.

But the contrariety of the traditional positions cannot simply be asserted without further examination. There are, in fact, three qualifications which must be made. The first of these is that it would not necessarily disprove the contrariety if Kant or Bentham or their followers were found appealing to some consideration other than desert or prevention respectively, since the consideration appealed to might be regarded as merely a subheading under desert or prevention. Kant's insistence that the Principle of Equality is the only principle by which manner and degree of punishment may be determined is predicated upon his belief that this Principle expresses the essence of punishing a man in accordance with his desert. The general point that it is only desert which is relevant might be true even if the Principle of Equality fails to stand up under scrutiny. And Bentham's rules for determining manner and degree of punishment are predicated upon Bentham's belief that it is by these rules alone that prevention may be made the criterion of justified punishment.

The second qualification is this: we must distinguish between two different ways in which Kant and Bentham could be offering these theses: as *descriptions* of what does in fact count in the justification of punishment, or as *prescriptions* concerning what ought to count. If the former, then their theses could be shown to be false by showing that in fact when judges or juries (lawyers or policemen, bystanders or reformers) set out to justify a particular case of punishment, or punishment as a practice, they appeal to considerations other than the preferred type; and the considerations they appeal to are not mere subheadings under the preferred type. Thus, if the retributivist thesis is a descriptive one, and it appears upon examination that in fact judges do not confine themselves to the question whether the sentence they pronounce is equal to what the criminal deserves, then the retributivist thesis is false. But if the retributivist thesis is a prescriptive one, then the retributivist would not agree that the judge had *justified* the sentence by appealing to these other considerations which are, he would hold, extraneous. "Justification," which we have yet to analyze, would then become a term to be applied not to just any process of giving reasons for punishment, but to an approved or warranted process. And of course the question would then become, What constitutes a process of reasoning properly approved or warranted?

If the traditional retributivists were offering their thesis as descriptive, and the traditional utilitarians were offering theirs as prescriptive, or *vice versa,* then the positions would not be contraries, for they would not be talking about the same thing, even though they were using the same form of language. But here we must enter yet another caution. For even if both utilitarian and retributivist were speaking prescriptively, they might still fail to come to grips, since there are at least two different kinds of prescription: logical and moral. One side might be insisting that the only *logically correct* way of justifying punishment is by appeal to his particular type of consideration; the other that the only *morally permissible* consideration is the type he espouses.

This is in fact the way a recent writer on the problem has tried to resolve it.[1] The retributivists, he contends, have only a logical point to make, whereas the utilitarian position is a moral one. So there is no genuine dispute between them. The retributivist is answering the question, "When (logically) *can* we punish?" The utilitarian is answering the question, "When (morally) *may* we or *ought* we to punish?" The answer to the retributivist's question is that we can *punish* a man only if he is guilty. The answer to the utilitarian's question is that we may punish a person only if punishment will have valuable consequences. The first answer consists in the elucidation of the use of the word "punish," the second in the expression of a moral stand. Those readers who have followed the exposition of the retributivist view in the first chapter will hardly need to be convinced that the retributivist can not be done away with so easily.[2] It should suffice to point out that the traditional retributivist is concerned not only with the "when," but also with the "how" and "how much" of punishment; and that in view of the tone of moral repugnance with which the utilitarian view is rejected by Kant and Bradley, the burden of proof is on him who would argue that the point being made is but a logical one about the use of the word, "punish."

Whether, leaving aside the matter of logical *vs.* moral prescriptiveness, the traditional positions fail to come to grips because one is asserting a descriptive and the other a pescriptive thesis, seems a difficult question to answer with certainty. It *can* be said, and we will examine the matter in some detail in later chapters, that neither position is in the least plausible, taken as a descriptive thesis. This is so obvious upon examination that it would seem implausible to attribute such a position to any thinker whose work has been of sufficient value to survive.

The third qualification on the thesis that retributivism and utilitarianism are contraries is this: we are speaking of *traditional* retributivism and utilitarianism, and in these positions there is failure to insist upon the different kinds of justificatory enterprise that may be underway in courtroom, legislative assembly, or reform meeting. Kant and Bentham, and their precursors and followers, tend to speak of the justification of punishment *simpliciter*, in a way we have still to examine in the next chapter.

But here, since we are still examining the traditional positions in their confrontation, we must speak of the justification of punishment *simpliciter* too. Our main business in this chapter will be to scrutinize the main arguments. It would hardly be worth while to examine every argument that has been hurled by one party at the other. This would be interesting to rhetoricians and antiquarians, perhaps, but would hardly carry us very far along the road to a reasoned view of punishment.

Many of the arguments used have been founded upon obvious misapprehension of the opposing position. Hegel is sometimes disposed of by holding that his position rests upon his metaphysics, which is said to be either inadequately grounded in evidence, or simply nonsensical. This is misdirected, as we have tried to show, since Hegel's arguments do not depend for their force upon acceptance of his metaphysical system, or even of metaphysics as an enterprise worthy of serious consideration. The utilitarian position is again and again attacked as if it rests on only one kind of prevention: reformation, or deterrence of the criminal, or deterrence of would-be criminals. These particular consequences are indeed given special emphasis by this utilitarian or that; but the utilitarian position does not stand or fall on the question whether reformation or deterrance is central.

Other arguments used are two-edged swords, cutting equally well in either direction. In this category are the arguments to the effect that retributivists (utilitarians) do not have an accurate rule for determining what punishment should be awarded; arguments hardly intelligible at all if the distinction is not made between legislative penalties and judicial sentences, and then not conclusive. Neither desert nor the public happiness can be set against a yardstick. Here also belong the more extreme arguments to the effect that desert (happiness) provides no standard at all for the determination of punishment because of internal conflicts in these standards. If it is true that the demands of justice seem sometimes to conflict with themselves, it is no less true that happiness and happiness can collide. A serious retributivist or utilitarian cannot fail to come to grips with the problem of how his standard is to be made less ambiguous; but the charge of ambiguity, directed either way, will hardly settle the issue!

We shall confine our analysis to two arguments in the traditional debate: the Punishment-of-the-Innocent Argument and the Revenge Argument. The former is directed against the utilitarians, the latter against the retributivists. They are the most frequently used arguments, and each is thought to be conclusive. A close examination of them can be instructive; for to meet them the utilitarian and retributivist must make some of the distinctions insisted upon in the next chapter. The point and the force of each position will become more apparent in the process.

The Punishment-of-the-Innocent Argument

I

The utilitarian is committed to doing whatever, in any given situation, is likely to promote public happiness; or if it is impossible to promote happiness, in the circumstances, at least to minimize unhappiness, and thus he is committed to the minimization of mischief, which is merely any state of affairs that brings about unhappiness. This means, so far as punishment is concerned, that he will punish when, and only when, and in such a way, and to the extent that, there is likely to be less mischief than if he did not punish, or punished in some other way.

But sometimes the best way to minimize mischief would be to punish an innocent man.[3]

Crime rate are notoriously sensitive to the swings of mass psychology: they wax and wane in popularity from time to time and from place to place. Let a particularly gruesome murder be committed in Fort Wayne, Indiana, and receive lurid coverage in the press, and the police will be on guard for an outbreak of similar murders from Chico, California, to Augusta, Maine. Crime rates vary also with the vagaries of the economic climate. Let there be wide-spread unemployment, combined with wide-spread economy-inspired cut-backs of security personnel in supermarkets and department stores; and there will be wide-spread theft. Cattle-rustling will increase with the price of meat, the economic circumstances of the rustlers remaining equal.

If the thesis that punishment of offenders deters other potential offenders is correct, then the greatest need for punishment is when offenses are on the up-swing of the cycle, or approaching it. Unfortunately it is not always easy to find someone to punish just when the crime wave is getting under way. And sometimes, by the nature of the circumstances, criminals are very hard to catch. Few law-enforcement officials may be available, or those present may be inadequately equipped (e.g., U.S. Coast Guard picket boats *vs* rum-running speedsters in prohibition times), or criminals may develop effective warning systems. The very nature of the offence may make apprehension difficult, as in theft by servants, vandalism, and the writing of threatening letters.

The time may be ripe for a deterrent example. A stiff prison term, an execution, could frighten would-be criminals, bring home to them the legal consequences of the crime they contemplate. And is the deterrent example less useful if the "criminal" is innocent, unbeknownst to all but the judge? Would not a consistent utilitarian judge sometimes be constrained by the principle of the minimzation of mischief to make use of misplaced punishment for the reduction of crime? How, as a utilitarian, could he *fail* to punish a man guilty in the eyes of everyone but himself, if an example were needed?[4]

This alleged consequence of the utilitarian position is so unwelcome that it constitutes one of the strongest arguments against the utilitarian theory of ethics in general, and opponents are held to be most conspicuously wrong when this implication of their doctrine of punishment is clearly made out.

The classic example of expression of the moral repulsion felt by the philosopher when he contemplates the punishment of the innocent is the passage, already quoted at length, from F. H. Bradley, and apparently directed against the philosophy of J. S. Mill. Here Bradley cries out that "if punishment is inflicted for any other reason whatever than because it is merited by wrong, it is a gross immorality, a crying injustice, an abominable crime, and not what it pretends to be."

The most obvious way to answer the charge that utilitarians would have to sanction punishment of the innocent, is to deny that the consequences of punishing an innocent man would ever be better than the consequences of not punishing him. This is argued by appealing to the extremely bad consequences of punishing an innocent man. These consequences, it is held, are so far-reaching and so superlatively bad in their total effect that it is impossible that it could ever be productive of the best consequences to punish an innocent man. Be the occasion what it may, the most that can be done by punishing an innocent man is to produce good consequences for a limited number of people over a limited span of time. But since punishing an innocent man subverts the very foundations of the system of law, and since without law human existence would be misery, the effects of punishing the innocent man extend farther and are more fraught with misery than the effects of not punishing him could ever be. No matter how pressing the reasons seem to be for punishing him, the good consequences of punishing him could not possibly extend as far as the bad ones. For in not punishing him, one is not subverting the system of law. In fact, to refuse to punish an innocent man, under circumstances in which excellent consequences would result from punishing him, is to give strong support to the system of law. The utilitarian may even go so far as to say that the greater the temptation to punish an innocent man, because of the excellent consequences which would result, the greater good is done in refusing to punish him and, instead, upholding the system of law.

The answer to this utilitarian defence is that it is simply false that the consequences of punishing an innocent are always worse than those of not doing so. There is no necessary connection between the punishment of the innocent and the subversion of law. *How* is the law supposed to be subverted? When do we say that the law is being subverted? The answer turns on what happens if it *is discovered* that a man has been punished for a crime of which he is not guilty. If it should come out in tomorrow morning's paper that, as a matter of policy, and this is necessary, a judge has sentenced an innocent man, for the purposes the judge deems good, what would be the effect of this news? It would be to lessen the respect of the people for the judiciary. When taken along with similar news, it has the effect that the argument that a given action is against the law has less weight: less and less, as the chances become greater and greater that one can be punished for what is not as well as for what is against the law. Termites have been allowed into the foundations.

But, the critic argues, all of this weakening of the foundations cannot take place unless the fact that an innocent man has been punished (knowingly) by the government is generally *known*. If it is *kept quiet* then the foundations are not weakened. So there is nothing wrong, on consistently utilitarian grounds, with punishing an innocent man, so long as it can be kept quiet.[5]

Against this, the utilitarian can argue the extreme difficulty of keeping the punishment of an innocent man quiet. For not only must the news be kept from the citizens but also from the officials of government, if subversion of the law is to be avoided. If officials hear that an official has punished an innocent for a seemingly good reason, then they are going to begin to feel free to punish men for what seem to them good reasons, even when men are not guilty; and the end of this is chaos.

But this answer still leaves open the possibility that there might be circumstances in which the judge could be very sure that only he knows that he is using an innocent man for exemplary purposes; and here the consistent utilitarian judge has no choice.

The defense from the extremely bad consequences of punishing the innocent shows at most that the utilitarian would *most of the time* not punish the innocent. But if he could keep it quiet he would punish the innocent whenever good seemed likely to result from it.

The argument may here be given an additional fillip. Not only would the utilitarian be occasionally committed to the approval of the punishment of the innocent; but he would also have to approve the reward of the guilty.

Suppose it is discovered by a group of distinguished psychiatrists that our approach to criminal conduct has been all wrong. To punish the man who has committed a crime has bad effects in several ways. Many criminals crave punishment, and it is because they crave it that they do the crime. Other criminals will be only further embittered and deranged by the punishment. With some criminals the crime is so compulsive that the threat of punishment has little or no deterrent effect.[6] But suppose that it is found that what *will* reduce the crime rate is to treat the criminal not harshly but sympathetically. Specifically it is found that what ought to be done is to give the criminal a chance to start life over under favorable auspices. Arguing from a successful experiment, it is held that if criminals are taken away from their former surroundings, given forty acres, a tractor, seed, and government support and advice for a period of two years, there is a good chance that they will become productive and peaceful citizens.

Let us now suppose that a hoodlum commits a violent and premeditated assault upon an innocent man. The hoodlum is duly examined and presented with his forty acres and tractor, and is carefully coached and nurtured by the government for two years. At the end of these two years, the program having succeeded, he has become a prosperous and active member of the Future Farmers of America, has built a neat home, and has bought two adjoining farms. At the end of twenty years he is the proprietor of a large estate on which blooded cattle roam between white fences, and has enrolled his daughter at Vassar.

Meantime, the victim of the assault has drifted from bad to worse. The injuries he has received from the criminal result in his losing his job, going on relief, in his loss of self-respect, in his living a life of loose wandering, and in his final reduction to selling pencils on a street corner. To top the example off in O. Henry style, we will suppose that the criminal now makes it a habit to buy his pencils from his victim, and that to soothe his conscience he pays his victim an additional ten cents per pencil.

This example has the anti-utilitarian advantage that the more successful the program is in reducing the crime rate by rehabilitating the criminal, the greater will be the injustice in the relative status of criminal and victim. The conclusion is that to show that a policy is justified on utilitarian grounds is not to show that it is morally justifiable; and that considerations of justice can conflict with considerations of utility.

Not only, then, the critic charges, will the utilitarian judge occasionally punish the innocent, but also he will from time to time reward the guilty. To punish an innocent or reward a guilty man seems the very paradigm of injustice; and, to the extent that we value justice, we seem unable to accept the utilitarian position insofar as it bears on punishment.

Even if it can be shown that the utilitarian judge would *very seldom* punish an innocent or reward a guilty man, he would not —we are sure—*refrain on principle* from such acts, for he has only one principle: the maximization of public happiness. Guided by this one principle he cannot but regard the prisoner before the bar as a possible lever for the public weal. But to make use of prisoners in this opportunistic way is to ignore the demands of justice. This is the center of gravity of the argument.

II

So far as the traditional utilitarian position is concerned, there is little more that can be said in reply to the punishment-of-the-innocent argument. The answer, if there is one, lies in a better understanding of utilitarianism than the traditional utilitarian

had. It rests on the distinction of levels of discussion to which we
have already referred. This distinction was first made clear by
contemporary philosophers not so much interested in taking sides
in the traditional dispute, as in the distinction itself. My references here will be to John Rawls' article, "Two Concepts of
Rules."[7]

The distinction as Rawls makes it, is between justifying a rule
or practice and justifying a particular action falling under it. The
first kind of justification, says Rawls, is the legislator's business,
and it turns mainly on utilitarian considerations. The legislator
is concerned with the question whether it would be best on the
whole to prohibit a certain kind of action, and how much it ought
to be penalized. The second kind is the business of the judge,
and it is settled by retributive-like arguments. The judge is not
qua judge entitled to consider whether it would be best on the
whole to punish a given kind of action, and he is severely limited
in his decision how and how much to punish. The judge's concern
is with the questions what the defendant has in fact done, and
whether that which he has done is against the law. Utilitarian
considerations are appropriate, then, to legislative discussions;
whereas retributive ones are appropriate to judicial discussions.
The apparent conflict between the two views is resolved by showing that "these views apply to persons holding different offices
and different duties, and situated differently with respect to the
system of rules that make up the criminal law."[8]

One possible objection to this resolution of the difficulty is
that utilitarianism if taken as the only principle of justification,
in legislative discussions, is likely to justify that which would be
"cruel and arbitrary." Even with the best of intentions, utilitarians
might find themselves favoring the infliction of suffering on innocent persons (whatever we want to call such infliction). Retributivists might insist that "there is no way to stop the utiliarian
principle from justifying too much except by adding to it a principle which distributes certain rights to certain individuals."[9]
This would be an abandonment of the strong position that it is
solely by reference to utility that punishment is justified in legislative discussions. Rawls says that the position need not be abandoned so quickly. For by concentrating on the distinction between
justifying rules and justifying actions falling under the rules, one
can see that the utilitarian legislator would be extremely unlikely

to favor the infliction of suffering on innocent individuals. *Qua* legislator, he does not make decisions about which particular individuals are to be made to suffer. What is he accused of, then? It must be of adopting the position that the institution of punishment, in which suffering is inflicted only on the guilty should be superceded by an institution in which it may be inflicted on the innocent as well. He is accused of wanting to change the whole system. But the ground on which he would favor abandoning punishment for a system in which the innocent may sometimes for good reason be made to suffer (Rawls calls this "Telishment"), would have to be that he thinks that the consequences of adopting Telishment would be better than the consequences of retaining Punishment. Telishment is the institution in which some group of officials has the right to decide under certain specified circumstances that it would be well to inflict suffering on ("telish") one or more persons who are innocent of the crime "for" which they are telished.[10]

But we have only to consider the probable consequences of such an institution to see that the utilitarian is extremely unlikely to favor it over punishment. These probable consequences are that, (a) since there is no real check on the officials who may telish, the right to telish will be abused for those officials' personal ends; and, (b) the deterrent effect of the penal system as a whole will be undermined, since a man may be telished even though he has not broken the law, and therefore when he is contemplating a crime, fear of the penalty does not provide the motive for refraining that it does in punishment.

This is, briefly, an answer which *could* be used by the utilitarian to defend himself against the "punishment-of-the-innocent" argument. It is a stronger defense than any offered by the traditional utilitarians, who themselves confused the distinction central to it, as I shall indicate below.

First, though, since I have discussed Rawls' position at some length, I should stop to say how I believe it should be qualified. Descriptively speaking, it is an everyday occurrence for judges to reason like utilitarians (though not over the question whether a man is guilty), and for legislators to reason like retributivists (though not over the question whether a particular person should be punished). If we wish to prescribe the relegation of retributivistic considerations to judicial discussion, and utilitarian considerations to legislative discussion, we must still offer arguments for doing so. And when we consider the matter more closely than Rawls need to do for his purpose, we find a variety of types of discussion under the headings: justifying rules, and justifying cases falling under them. Some of these will be mentioned in the next chapter.

III

It is easy enough to see how Bradley could have accused J. S. Mill of advocating a position which would commit him to the punishment of the innocent upon occasion. There are passages in *An Examination of The Philosophy of Sir William Hamilton* such as the following:

> . . . whoever cultivates a disposition to wrong, places his mind out of sympathy with the rest of his fellow creatures, and if they are aware of his disposition, becomes a natural object of their active dislike. He not only forfeits the pleasure of their good will, and the benefit of their good offices . . . but he also renders himself liable to whatever they may think necessary to do in order to protect themselves against him; which may probably include punishment, as such, and will certainly involve much that is equivalent in its operation on himself.[11]

Mill is obviously here talking about the justification of punishment. His words are certainly open to the interpretation that in individual cases in which a man has a "disposition to wrong" his "fellow creatures" (*which* fellow creatures?) may treat him in "whatever way they think necessary": apparently even if on that particular occasion he is not guilty of breaking a law. Bradley's criticism points up an ambiguity in Mill's remarks about punishment. Would Mill, confronted with this ambiguity, have chosen to say that utilitarian considerations are relevant in justification of findings of guilt? This seems, to say the least, doubtful. To Hamilton's free will doctrine, Mills replies, "The question deemed to be so puzzling is, how punishment can be justified, if men's actions are determined by motives, among which motives punishment is one. A more difficult question would be, how it can be justified if they were not so determined."[12] Punishment could not very well be a motive in a system in which the innocent are punished as well as the guilty.

An interesting historical footnote to the punishment-of-the-

innocent argument is provided by Bradley's latest paper on punishment, "Some Remarks on Punishment," which appeared eight-
een years after *Ethical Studies,* which we have quoted above.[13]
In this paper, Bradley struggles with some misgivings about punishment which are brought about by reflection on what he takes
to be the ethical consequences of Darwin's discoveries. The gist
of Bradley's reflections is this: Human beings, unlike animals, can
mark out their own goals and lay plans for achieving them. A
fundamental goal is the production of a "better" race of men than
we have now. This would automatically come about if it were
not for artificial human restrictions on competition. If it were
not for these restrictions, there would be a survival of the fittest
(best) men, and a weeding out of the unfit (worst). But we
have moral scruples which make us spare the lives of the utterly
useless and even of the dangerous. We do not even have the intelligence to do what we obviously ought to do if we are to take
our providence into our own hands: that is to refuse to take upon
ourselves the useless burden of raising abnormal and weak off-
spring of the "morally unfit," and supporting the morally unfit
themselves. One of the first axioms of social ethics is that the
state has the right to cut off its own "weak and rotten parts." This
is a corollary of the right the state has to ensure its own survival.

Now this cutting off of the weak and rotten parts, Bradley
calls "social (sometimes "Moral") Surgery." And Bradley feels
that the obvious need for social surgery somehow undermines but
does not overthrow his former position about punishment. It undermines it because it seems to require us to place the stamp of
approval on some cases of punishment of the innocent.

> . . . how does Darwinism alter our views and threaten moral
> revolution? It tends, in a word, to break the connection between
> punishment and guilt. . . . The union of these ideas is in fact so
> rational and strong that in the end perhaps we have no choice
> but to respect it nominally.[14]

We are forced to agree that even though it may be unjust to
punish the innocent, in some special cases we ought to do it.
But on the other hand, Bradley does not feel that the need for
social surgery requires him to change his former position in any
really fundamental respect. The reason for this is that Bradley
is aware that *if utilitarian considerations enter into the deter-*

mination of "guilt," then what we have is no longer punishment.
So in the end he allows room for a distinction between "strict"
punishment and social surgery.

> We may doubt if such cutting-off without crime can fairly be
> called punishment, but the thing being justified, I will not pause
> to consider the name.[15]
> All that is required is that (if pressed) we should admit that
> such a modified penalty is not strict punishment.[16]

Once this distinction is made, there is no difficulty. It was only
Bradley's hesitance about whether to think of social surgery as
punishment which had created the difficulty.

IV

We now turn to the charge that the consistent utilitarian
would, under certain circumstances, have to approve the reward
of the guilty; where to reward the guilty would be manifestly
unjust when the state of the rewarded criminal is compared to
the state of the criminal's victim. Let us examine this charge in
the same way in which we examined the charge that the utilitarian favors the punishment of the innocent. What is being proposed does not refer to this or that particular case, but to a practice. The practice must now be more fully specified. We are not
given the details but must speculate about what they would be.
Let us therefore speculate as follows: The system is such that
when a man is suspected of doing that which the law prohibits
he is brought before a "judge." The "judge" decides whether in
fact the defendant has committed a crime. If the defendant has
committed a crime, the "judge" declares him guilty. Now it may
be that in being found guilty the criminal becomes automatically
subject to a "penalty": namely, that he is given forty acres and a
tractor, the size of the farm perhaps varying with the seriousness
of the offense. Or it may be that the "judge" is given discretion to
award whatever other aid will in his opinion be best calculated
to rehabilitate the offender and keep the offender's name off the
police blotter in the future.

Whether to grant or refuse the name "Punishment" to this
institution is not essential to the utilitarian's argument. The only
question is whether a consistent utilitarian would be likely to
adopt it as a practice. The answer is that, since the utilitarian is

interested not only in the reformation of criminals but also in the deterrence of others from committing crime; he certainly would be unlikely to accept any such practice. Instead of minimizing mischief he would be positively inviting it. "But by hypothesis, the practice in question will, if followed, reduce the crime rate!" This, then, on closer examination, seems a strange hypothesis. What state of affairs must we picture in which such a practice would succeed in reducing crime? A state in which social pressure is sufficient to restrain all but compulsive criminals? But if this were the case then the objection to the practice would disappear. For if all "criminals" are really persons who need rehabilitation before they can gain control over their own actions, then there does not seem any injustice in rehabilitating these persons rather than punishing them. To the extent that the population is able, given knowledge of a penalty, to refrain from that the doing of which is penalized, then the penalty would seem to serve the utilitarian better than "reward."

Utilitarianism (the utilitarian could insist) can be understood as a justification of practices; and the very understanding of what it is that is being defended entails an understanding about practice-rules. For if the practice is to *be* the practice under defense, then it cannot be at the same time some other practice which may not be defensible. Punishment is one way of conducting human affairs. If *this* is what is being defended, there is no question of "punishing" the innocent.

Now let us turn to the main assault upon the retributivist position.

The Revenge Argument

V

Retributivists are often, and in a variety of ways, accused of wishing to have revenge upon the criminal, and deceiving themselves and others by disguising this wish as a demand of justice. This accusation is seldom elaborated into an argument; though there does seem to be an argument implicit in it. It is that since the retributivist explicitly ignores the consideration of the question whether any good consequences may be expected from punishment, and yet insists on the right to punish where a crime has been committed, his position is morally indistinguishable from that of a man who simply insists on revenge for crime.

The retributivist is committed to the position that it would sometimes be morally right to punish a man even though no good consequence should result: even though the consequence of punishing would be positively and extremely harmful. Suppose a person commits a crime, and the commission of the crime is a relatively minor moral offense. Say he is Paul, a fifteen-year-old, and he takes an automobile for a "joy ride," intending to return it. Suppose also that Paul has had mental difficulties and is under the care of a psychiatrist. Suppose the psychiatrist is reasonably sure that if he is allowed to continue treatment of Paul for only six months longer, he will be completely readjusted to normal life; and that if he is sent to a reformatory for his crime he will suffer a severe set-back and will become permanently mentally disabled. Does one have a moral right to send Paul to the reformatory? But would not a retributivist who thinks that the reformatory term is "equal" to the crime have to approve of sending Paul to the reformatory? He cannot take into account what the consequences might be for Paul. But is it not clear here that to rely solely on retributive considerations is to promote injustice?

When a man is punished, it is trivial to say, he suffers pain or he is deprived of that which he does not want to be deprived of. The general problem of the justification of punishment can be made to arise by combining this observation with the observation that unless one man has a justification for depriving the other of a thing or for causing him to suffer pain; then the deprivation or the pain-causing is wrong. The retributivist will say: "I cause the man pain because he has done what is wrong."[17] But this is so far hardly sufficient. How has the pain been *related* to the wrong-doing? We have here two separate events. How does the reference to the first make the second right? This is not clear. And it will not do for the retributivist to add "Not only has he done what is wrong, but I have authority over him." For this begs the question or it is irrelevant. If it is claimed that the retributivist has *moral* authority (a right) to do what he does, then he begs the question. If it is claimed that he is in a position of legal authority over the person on whom pain has been inflicted, does not the question about the moral right to inflict the pain still remain unanswered? To say "He committed a crime," and to add "I have authority over him" is simply not sufficient. Because situations can arise in which these statements may be true, but in which, yet, punishment will *do no good,* and in which, as in our example, it will *do positive harm.*

To give as one's *reason* for inflicting pain or deprivation on a man that he has done a certain thing is an all too familiar way of talking. This is the language of revenge. "Why did you ambush John Hatfield?" "That's what *he* did to Harold McCoy!"; "Why did you blackball my candidate?" "You did it to mine!" The suspicion is confirmed that retributivism is revenge-taking in disguise when we note how naturally revenge-taking assumes the form of the "Principle of equality": ambush the ambusher, blackball the blackballer. The retributivist has not shown how the connection is to be made between the reference to what the man punished has done, and the punishment; but the connection is all too clear. To show why action is taken against the man, and to explain why that particular kind of action was chosen, it is sufficient to show what the man has done, *if* what is being shown is that one's action is simple retaliation. For retaliation must be *for* something and it must be appropriate to that which it is for. The mystic connection which Hegel sees between crime and punishment has very real historical and emotional roots.

Kant's theory of punishment, says Westermarck,[18] is "simply an expression of the emotion of moral resentment of a more primitive type than that which is embodied in the criminal legislation of our own time." In our own time we offer reformation and deterrence as reasons for punishment. But these are really just rationalizations. Punishment is most fundamentally revenge-taking. And, Westermarck could have added, the retributivist practically acknowledges it; in this respect he is to be preferred to the utilitarian. Says Westermarck, "It is one of the most interesting facts relating to the moral consciousness of the most humane types, that it in vain condemns the gratification of the very desire from which it sprang. It reminds one of the man of low extraction who, in spite of all acquired refinement, still bears his origin stamped on his face."[19] "The criminal law," says Sir James Stephen, "stands to the passion of revenge in much the same relation as marriage to the sexual appetite."[20] And O. W. Holmes, Jr. says, in *The Common Law,* "It certainly may be argued with some force, that it has never ceased to be one object of punishment to satisfy the desire for vengeance."[21] Westmarck[22] and Hobhouse[23] agree in tracing the origin of criminal law back to simple retaliation for wrong. Some psychiatrists are convinced that the *real* reason for punishment is the desire for revenge. Menninger tells us, "The reasons usually given to justify punishment do not explain why it exists. They serve only to conceal the truth, that the scheme of punishment is a barbaric system of revenge, by which society tries to "get even" with the criminal."[24]

Admittedly we have here a line of argument which attacks both the retributivist and the utilitarian positions. But, the critic argues, does not the retributivist have much the worst of it? For whereas the utilitarian can claim that deterrence and reform really are *reasons* for punishment, and not simple rationalization of the desire for revenge on the criminal; does not the retributivist completely lack a denfense? He *says* there is *no* reason for punishment other than that the man punished *has done what he has done*. But this is the very "reason" that Hatfield gives when he takes revenge on McCoy: How can the retributivist distinguish between specifying why one wants revenge, and giving one's reason for punishing?

What has been called in question is not the retributivist's claim that ill desert is a necessary condition of just punishment; but the contention that it is a sufficient one. It is the rejection of other considerations which bear on the rightness or wrongness of punishment of which the retributivist is accused. In the person of Kant he says that all such considerations should be rigorously excluded.

Let us first examine the way in which the traditional retributivist could meet the revenge argument: "could," because I have not found an explicit defense of the traditional view.

First, arguments about the origin and emotional basis of retributivism prove nothing about the validity of that position. If the institution of punishment has developed out of private revenge-taking, is it not an advance over that practice? It certainly does not follow that what developed from a given practice *is* that very same practice. And if the institution is reinforced by emotions which if not institutionally expressed would be socially deleterious, is this an argument against the institution?

Second, the retributivist could say, he cannot be held responsible for the regrettable fact that, no matter what philosophy of legislation may govern, there will be hard cases. But for the example of Paul to count as an argument against retributivism, it must be shown that this is more than a special case involving hardship. Such cases arise for utilitarians too. Paul's age and mental condition are data for the retributivist judge as much as for the utilitarian one. They bear on the degree of his guilt, if he is to be held guilty at all.

Third, why would a retributivist judge be more likely than a utilitarian one to ignore the effects of punishment? He is trying to make the punishment proportionate to the crime. Is it not open to him to place on his balance-scale the near-by and remote consequences of the sentence, and to take these into account as a part of the punishment? If it is reasonable to suppose that permanent injury will be done by a reformatory sentence, then this possibility becomes as much a part of the calculus of retribution as of utility.

Fourth, the resemblance between language of retributivism and the language of McCoy is only a surface resemblance. Indeed, Kant says that it is just because the criminal X-ed that he must be X-ed; but this is only the outcropping of a theory with deep foundations, involving a conception of freedom and its protection, of the dignity of the individual including the dignity of the criminal, and of the universal nature of the criminal's act when it is regarded as rational.

But the retributivist has not yet met the gravamen of the revenge argument. It is that the very theorizing about justice, freedom, and human dignity is what lies on the surface: that these are but glosses over the demand for revenge. Even if the retributivist would treat Paul in the very same way as the utilitarian, he would do so with the wrong motive. His very meticulousness in balancing the punishment against the crime is evidence of the revenge-inspired nature of the procedure. The retributivist has been challenged to produce a criterion by means of which we can say that A is punishing from motives of justice, but that B is punishing from motives of revenge. How are we to distinguish Solomon from Hatfield, if both can speak the language of theory?

To meet the gravamen of the charge, the retributivist must make and insist upon some distinctions not often made by traditional retributivists and never insisted upon. Who is it that is being accused of harboring revenge? Is it the retributivist judge, legislator, or advocate of the institution of punishment? A judge, be he retributivist or not, must find a man guilty *of* something and sentence him *for* something. This is but the other side of the coin we examined in our discussion of the punishment-of-the-innocent argument. The judge may refer only to what has been done, but if so he speaks elliptically, for part of his justification is surely that what has been done is prohibited and carries a legal penalty. Such backward-looking use of language is not therefore enough to convict the judge of a desire for vengeance.[25] Legislators' legal threats are hypothetical ones, directed against persons they cannot know by name; and defenders of the institution of punishment may be defending it precisely on the ground that it rules out vengeance-taking as a practice.[26]

VI

That the traditional arguments examined do not remove the impasse between the traditional positions should now be obvious. The traditional positions are, with the qualifications we noted, contraries. Even if the punishment-of-the-innocent argument were successful against the traditional utilitarian position it would not follow that retributivism is true; and *vice versa* for the revenge argument. And the arguments are only successful, at best, against the traditional forms of the retributivist and utilitarian positions: forms in which crucial distinctions between different sorts of punishment-justification are not made.

The utilitarian can defend himself against the punishment-of-the-innocent argument by distinguishing between discussions of practices and discussions falling within, presupposing, those practices. The retributivist can defend himself against the revenge argument by distinguishing between a person who is playing the role of judge or legislator, and a person not playing a role but merely seeking revenge. As we begin to recognize the variety of contexts within which punishment can be challenged and defended we move toward a new interpretation of retributivism and utilitarianism. For they can tell us what can or cannot, ought or ought not to count as a reason in the justification of punishment;

but the justification of punishment takes place in a variety of contexts from a variety of standpoints, which must now be distinguished.

CHAPTER II

FOOTNOTES

1. A. M. Quinton, "On Punishment," *Analysis,* June 1954, pp. 133-42.
2. The inadequacy of this view has been well exposed by other writers and need not be dealt with in detail here. Cf. esp. K. G. Armstrong, "The Retributivist Hits Back," *Mind,* LXX(1961), pp. 471-90.
3. This argument is usually directed against that wider form of utilitarianism which takes as its principle the promotion of consequences "good on the whole," but, for simplicity, I confine this statement of it to a form uniform with the Benthamite utilitarianism described in Chapter I.
4. The argument, if stated in its most general form, would emphasize "misplaced" punishment: punishment inflicted in such a way as to fall on the wrong shoulders, or too hard on the right ones. Thus there would be included, besides simple punishment of an innocent man, group punishment for an individual's crime, punishment for crimes not yet committed but expected, and punishment of the guilty for more henious crimes than they actually committed. An analogous argument concerns reward of the guilty. Bentham saw the problem in its general form, and discussed it under the heading "Of Mis-seated Punishment" in *Principles of Penal Law,* Pt. II, Book IV.
5. On the argument that a utilitarian would have to approve punishment of the innocent—on occasion—so long as it can be kept quiet, see especially Mr. Mabbott's well-known "Excursus on Indirect Utilitarianism" in his paper, "Punishment," Mind, XLVIII, 1939, pp. 155-57. This article is one of the best things on punishment written in the last thirty years.
6. The psychiatrist's argument against punishment will be examined in more detail in Chapter VI.
7. *Philosophical Review,* January 1955, pp. 3-32.
8. *Ibid.,* p. 6.
9. *Ibid.,* p. 9.
10. Strictly speaking, we should not use the words "innocent" and "guilty" in speaking of the institution of telishment, for to say that a man is innocent is to say that he is not liable to punishment, but not to say that he is not liable to telishment. If we should elaborate the new institution we might use "innocel" and "guiltel." To say that a man is "innocel" is to say that (a) he did not break the law, and (b) it would not be best on the whole to telish him. To say that he is "guiltel" is to say that (since there must be some connection with the "crime") (a) he had the motive and the opportunity to commit the "crime," and (b) the proper authorities have, under the prescribed circumstances, decided that it would be best on the whole to have him "telished" "for" that "crime."
11. *An Examination of The Philosophy of Sir William Hamilton,* London, 1865, p. 508.
12. *Ibid.,* p. 510.
13. *International Journal of Ethics,* 1894, pp. 269-84, reprinted in *Collected Essays,* Oxford, 1935, Vol. I, pp. 146-64.
14. *Ibid.,* p. 273.
15. *Ibid,* p. 275.
16. *Ibid.,* p. 284, n. 1.

17. That this argument does not take into account the subtlety of Kant's defence need hardly be mentioned.
18. *Ethical Relativity*, New York, 1932, p. 288.
19. *Ibid.*, p. 86.
20. *General View of the Criminal Law of England*, p. 99.
21. *The Common Law*, Boston, 1881, p. 40.
22. *Op. cit.*, pp. 62-86.
23. *Morals in Evolution*, New York, 1929, Chapter III.
24. Karl Menninger, *The Human Mind*, New York, 1945, p. 448.
25. This point will be expanded in Chapter IV.
26. This point will be expanded in Chapter V.

SOME SORTINGS-OUT

Clarity, too, I know, has been said to be not enough; but perhaps it will be time to into that when we are within measurable distance of achieving clarity on some matter.

J. L. AUSTIN, *A Plea for Excuses*

When traditional retributivists and utilitarians speak of "punishment" there is no single thing to which their words always refer. They group together, by default of distinction, a variety of practices and institutions, and a variety of situations which can arise within these practices or institutions. "The" question of the purpose of punishment can be made intelligible only if we have done something to specify what things are under discussion, and from what standpoints.

I

One way to get at the different questions involved in "the" question of the purpose of punishment is to note the ambiguities involved in statements about that purpose. Bradley tells us that ". . . if punishment is inflicted for any other reason whatever than because it is merited by wrong, it is a gross immorality. . . ."[1] Mill contends that the "two ends which on the Necessitarian Theory, are sufficient to justify punishment" are "the benefit of the offender himself, and the protection of others."[2] Ross holds that "A Utilitarian theory . . . if it justifies punishment at all, is bound to justify it solely on the grounds of the effects it produces."[3] Kant, Hegel, and Bentham speak of what does and does not justify punishment.

What, exactly, is the referent of the word "punishment" in these passages? Does it include that which fathers inflict on children, which supernatural beings visit on humans, or which humans inflict on other humans in the name of supernatural beings?[4] How does it include them? As conjuncts? As disjuncts? Or are we, as is more likely, speaking only of legal punishment? What holds for legal punishment does not necessarily hold for each of the other institutions and practices of punishment with which we are familiar; and certainly does not hold for mere vengeance-taking or wanton harm.

And is the person speaking of the justification of punishment speaking *of* the institution or *from within it,* as the bearer of one of its roles. Who is advocating punishment? Who is being punished? Is the person recommending punishment assuming the position of a judge, a legislator, an attorney? Is the person punished one who has committed a legal offence, one who has not but might, a group of persons jointly held responsible for a crime? At what stage of the game is it recommended that desert, deterrence, reformation be taken as decisive of whether or not and how and how much to punish? When a legislator is discussing what penalty to attach to legal prohibition? After the judge has found the defendant guilty?

It would be incorrect and unfair to claim that some of these distinctions cannot be found in the writings of the authors taking up one or other of the traditional positions we have examined. But they are not insisted upon; they are given at best passing recognition. Yet these distinctions are right at the center of the issue. How are we to decide between retributivists and utilitarians (or between utilitarian sectarians) unless we know what is the question at issue? The first order of business must surely be to remove the ambiguity from our discussion of the purpose of punishment.

As a beginning we shall assume that it is the institution of legal punishment which is central in the writings of our chief protagonists; not parental punishment, or revenge feuds, or the wearing of hair shirts, or social ostracism, or eternal damnation,[4] or the training of animals, or the disciplining of troops. The hopelessness of resolving a discussion of "punishment" where the word can slide from one of these possible referents to others should be obvious.

As an illustration of the very different practices involved, and by way of introduction to the concept of legal punishment, consider the contrast between legal and parental punishment. If we are speaking of legal punishment, then it is legitimate to object that Jones was not punished, but only harmed, if he was not duly sentenced by a judge. But it does not follow that Johnny was only harmed for pouring ink on the oriental rug if he was not sentenced by a judge. In Legal Punishment, there is no particular person who punishes the offender. If I am told that a child was punished for biting his brother, it makes sense to ask, "Who punished him?" But if I am told that the man who robbed the bank has received a punishment of life imprisonment, it does not make sense for me to ask, "Who punished (is punishing) him?" and expect the name or title of some person. It might be said that the State, or that Society punished him. But it is only in a Pickwickian sense that the warden is punishing him by keeping him in the prison to which the judge has committed him; though the warden might punish him for trying to escape. And, though the judge found him guilty of a crime to which a range of penalties is attached, and chose one of the penalties in passing sentence, it sounds odd to say that the judge punished the robber. This is not to say that in Legal Punishment people are somehow punished without being punished *by* anyone. It is only to say that the question who did (is doing) the punishment does not arise.[5]

II

We have referred to legal punishment both as a practice and as an institution. "Practice" is the wider term, and includes everything we would call an institution. To have a practice is to have a set or standard way of dealing with a recurrent situation. I *make it my practice* to take along a raincoat if the weather is threatening as I start for my office. But the reference is to social practices. It *is the practice* that when one man uses the words, "I promise," under certain conditions which are well understood (he knows what he is saying, is not under drugs, compelled at gunpoint, etc.) he is expected to do that which he promises to do, on pain of violating a serious obligation. We have practices according to which automobiles meeting at an intersection, or ships meeting at sea, are governed; practices for the conducting of meetings; practices for the tracing of family relationships; for the timing and location of our meals; for the marking of time; for the measurement of distance; for the allocation of goods (standing in line, bidding); governing the playing of games. Not to have a practice is to meet each situation anew, and decide how to cope with it. I do not make it my practice to buy a fishing license each January, because I may or may not go fishing in the following year; whereas a commercial fisherman or enthusiastic amateur does have this practice. There is no practice governing right-of-way in a deep, narrow channel, for submerged vessels meeting head-on. But if the number of submarines and narrow deep channels should increase, a practice would develop.

But we do not speak only of "making x our practice" or to the effect that "the practice is x." We also speak of "the practice of x," where x is not a variable for some bit of recurrent behavior, but a name, like marriage, baseball, contracting, chess, kidnapping, promising, willing (as in the making of wills), inheritance, slavery, divorce, voting, bidding, christening, tipping, mourning, or punishment. In this use of "practice" the situation is more complex than in that referred to by a simple description of what people in fact do, as in "the practice is to pass to the right," "the practice is to wear dark clothes," "the practice is to have breakfast at eight." To understand the practice of voting, e.g., is to understand a complex of behavior, not just an action which could be ordered or directed or advised without further explanation. A child can be cautioned to say "thank you" for meals given him more easily than he can be advised that he is not eligible to vote or marry. But it is not merely a matter of relative complexity; contracting and marrying have, as we shall see, a different logical status from passing to the right and saying "thank you."

Some practices of this more complex and logically distinct sort are also referred to as institutions. We speak of the institutions of marriage, the law, private property, representative government, and the family. Punishment is often referred to as an institution. The distinction between complex practices in general and those we refer to as institutions seems to be mainly a matter of degree of complexity and of importance. Practices of great complexity, articulated into subpractices, and considered of great importance, are institutions. Baseball is not of sufficient importance to be an institution though it is sufficiently complex. Promising is not sufficiently complex. Bidding, divorce, and voting are subpractices which can be understood only by reference to the institutions of private property, marriage, and representative government; and are therefore not institutions in their own right. Punishment is probably a borderline case. Indeed, it can be understood only by reference to the institution of the law; but it may be a point at issue whether it is necessarily "included in" the institution of law.

An advantage of referring to the institution, rather than to the practice, of punishment is that then we might not confuse two very different sorts of thing we mean by practice. Though institutions are all complex practices, complex practices differ importantly from simple ones. Simple practices can be described in such terms as "wearing dark clothes," "passing to the right;" complex practices cannot. To learn what it is to punish or vote or bid we must learn an articulated pattern of action involving roles, concepts, and rules.[6]

In learning about legal punishment, we learn a complex way of behaving, centered around such seemingly simple concepts as *judge, law,* and *guilt.* A concept can be taken, for our purposes, as the way a word is used.[7] When, as a child, I made a mistake about the way the word "guilty" is used, made the mistake consistently, and not merely by chance, this was not so much evidence that my concept of *guilt* was confused as the criterion of such confusion. When my parents corrected me in my mistakes, they were teaching me about the institution of legal punishment.

Thinking of a concept as the way a word is used suggests an approach to the notion of that complex sort of practice we call an institution, by comparing the way a child learns an institutional concept and the way he learns other words. Consider the words "guilty" and "ball." We can conceive of a child who does not know how to use any other word but "ball;" but we cannot conceive of a child who does not know how to use any other word than "guilty." For when we say that a child "knows how to use the word 'guilty'," one of the things we mean is that he gets the relations right between the use of this word and words like "judge," "jail," and "crime." We explain to children that those men carrying rifles are *guards,* and the other men in uniform are *convicts* who have committed a *crime* like *robbery* or *murder*; that they have been *tried* and found *guilty*; and that the *judge* has then sentenced them to *imprisonment* in a *penitentiary.* We cannot explain to a child the use of any one of these terms without making use of some of the others. We cannot explain *arresting* to a child by showing him a man in blue uniform placing handcuffs on a man who wears no uniform. If a child has not learned the use of "ball," we continue to show him balls, and to contrast these with melons, light bulbs, bats, and rackets. We compare and point out until he learns. But if he has not learned the use of "guilty," supposing, for example, that a policeman can declare a man guilty, we must rehearse with him the connections between "guilt" and a set of cognate terms. And the more we rehearse this with him, the tighter we weave the net of concepts: the more precise we make the relations between them.

To attempt a "complete" definition of such a complex institution, and one subject to so many variations, as legal punishment, would be to overdo our ground survey by hacking through a jungle we would do better to view from a distance. If we are to consider the purpose of punishment, we need a definition which is sufficiently general to include a large number of variants. Otherwise, as Hart has pointed out,[8] debates about punishment can be closed off too easily and soon by disclaiming the institution under attack. On the other hand, (to keep us aware that we *are* going to walk a tightrope) let us bear in mind that the definition must be sufficiently particular to rule out parental punishment, treatment, and other practices *not* under debate. It should go without saying, also, that we do not want to define legal punishment in such a way as to tip the scale in favor of retributivism or utilitarianism. We want to avoid allowing any part of the justification (or dis-justification) of punishment to creep into its definition, so that a case for acceptance or rejection or reform can seem to turn on "the very meaning" of punishment.[9]

III

"Legal Punishment," as I shall use the term, will refer to an institution having the following three characteristics:

1. There must be a system of threats, officially promulgated, that should given legal rules be violated, given consequences generally regarded as unpleasant will be inflicted upon the violator.

2. The threatened unpleasant consequences must be inflicted

only upon persons tried and found guilty of violating the
rules in question, and only for the violation of the rules.

3. The trial, finding of guilt, and imposition and administration of the unpleasant consequences must be by authorized
agents of the system promulgating the rules violated.

Certain explanatory comments are needed; and these may be
taken as a part of my definition.

(1) Threats may be either categorical ("I am going to do
such and such to you.") or hypothetical ("If you do so and so,
I will do such and such to you.") The threats in question are
hypothetical ones. Threats may also be directed to particular,
nameable, individuals; or to any individual who meets a given
anonymous description. Descriptions may define classes of persons who can be named and listed (the citizens of London, the
members of the Conrad family), or classes of persons who cannot
be named and listed (the driver approaching from the right,
anyone committing armed robbery, a person carrying a concealed
weapon). We shall refer to this latter type of description as an
anonymous description.[10]

The threat, then, is of the form, "If anyone does so and so, then
such and such will follow." The "such and such" to follow may
be explicitly or only vaguely made out. But there must be *some*
indication or tacit understanding of what is being threatened.
This rules out, as Legal Punishment, Gilbert and Sullivan's institution, in which there is a Lord High Executioner completely
free to apply his ingenious and unpredictable imagination to the
task of making "the punishment fit the crime."

The authority promulgating the rules and the threats attached
to them may be, so far as this definition is concerned, a King,
Dictator, Tribal Leader, Governor, Council of Elders, Legislature,
or what have you. Promulgation may be by verbal edict, town
criers, posting on the door of the Palace, or publication in official
journals; and the rule promulgated may or may not already have
been in common use. Authority may be derived from appoint-
ment, descent, designation by a supernatural being, election, or
any other source. All that is necessary is that the source of authority and the derivation process be generally accepted as genuine. For convenience, we shall refer to the authority promulgating rules and threats as the Legislator, and the authority

applying them as the Judge. It is not *necessary* that the Legislator or Judge should be eligible to fulfill the anonymous description of the crime, even if it is desirable that institutions of legal punishment should have this characteristic.

The unpleasant consequences threatened must be such that almost everyone wishes to avoid them as involving pain, suffering, embarrassment, inconvenience, or loss; even though some eccentrics may regard them as sources of pleasure, pride, salvation, or public recognition.

(2) and (3). There is, so to speak, a regulated monopoly of the unpleasant consequences in question vested in the officials authorized to use them. They may be used by those officials only according to due process of law; and they may not be used at all in the private affairs of the people.

IV

Even such a brief overview of the institution of Legal Punishment should serve to remind us that there are a variety of contexts within which the question about the purpose or rationale of punishment can arise. A discussion about the purpose of punishment in a courtroom is very different from a discussion about the purpose of punishment in a legislative assembly. And questions about the purpose of the institution, which includes courtrooms and legislative assemblies, are something yet again. To be more specific, here are some of the questions which could be under discussion:

Judicial Level

1. Should A be punished at all? (Is he guilty?)
2. Should A be punished this way? (Ten years, transportation)

Legislative Level

3. Should this kind of thing (euthanasia) be punished?
4. Should this crime (perjury) be punished this way? (Ten to twenty years)

"Reform" Level

5. Should anybody ever be punished this way? (Executed, imprisoned)

6. Should anybody ever be punished? (Should we abolish punishment?)

Usually it is not necessary to specify what the question is that the speaker has in mind when he claims that punishment does or does not serve its purpose. The role of the speaker (judge, legislator, prosecutor, prisoner), the state of the proceedings (after the verdict, before the sentence), the occasion (a legislative discussion about capital punishment, the appeal of a case from a lower court) are ordinarily enough to inform us what kind of discussion is taking place. If the judge, addressing himself to the criminal, in passing sentence, asserts that the criminal has done a very wicked thing and that he will benefit from a prison term; then the judge is offering justification for the severe sentence he is about to pronounce, in terms of the purposes which he believe sentences by judges should serve. This justification will not be confused by the defendant's lawyer with the justification for the finding of guilt, nor with the justification of the legal penalty in accordance with which the criminal is sentenced. If he *should* be guilty of such confusion, his remarks would be ignored, or ruled out as irrelevant.

The philosopher is not in such a happy position. The context does not make the bearing of his remarks immediately obvious. He has taken the concept of punishment, as it were, to the dissecting table; and in that antiseptic atmosphere it is a corpse without family connections. But punishment, the corpse, has no purpose; it is only punishment for this crime, or penalties attached to crimes, or institutions, which are purposeful. The quest for the purpose of punishment, without the explanations or indications which allow us to *place* it, is not likely to be fruitful.

CHAPTER III

FOOTNOTES

1. F. H. Bradley, *Ethical Studies*, Second Edition, Oxford, 1927, pp. 26-7.
2. *An Examination of Sir William Hamilton's Philosophy*, London, 1865, p. 510.
3. W. D. Ross, *The Right and The Good*, Oxford, 1930, p. 56.
4. For an interesting discussion of the right of God to inflict eternal punishment for sins committed in a "time-bound" world, Cf. especially Augustine, *Confessions*, VII, III; City of God, XII, VII; and Aquinas, *Summa Theologica*, I-II, Q. 87. For the thesis that rulers derive their right to punish from Divine authority, Cf. Malebranche, *Traite de Morale*, II, XI; and Hawkins,

Rev., J. D. B., "Punishment and Moral Responsibility," in O'Sullivan (ed.) *The King's Good Servant*, Oxford, 1948, pp. 92-98.

5. This feature of Legal Punishment much intrigues Tolstoy, (Cf. *Resurrection*).

6. By a "role" we mean a certain type of concept, one which refers to a class of persons who meet a certain general description, such as *legislator* or *convict*. "Rule" is an intuitively simple and analytically fearsome concept which we would do better to leave to the reader's intuitive understanding; mentioning only that it concerns the common understanding of what is required of role-players in certain standard situations.

7. I would not wish to defend this precept (any more than Wittgenstein did) to the uttermost. But it does suggest a useful mode of analysis.

8. H. L. A. Hart, "Prolegomena to The Principles of Punishment," The Presidential Address of the Aristotelian Society, *Proceedings of the Aristotelian Society*, 1959-60.

9. In drafting the definition to follow, I have been greatly helped by Hart's article, and by other excellent articles recently published. Cf. especially A. Flew, "The Justification of Punishment," *Philosophy*, 1954, pp. 291-307; S. I. Benn, "An Approach to the Problems of Punishment," *Philosophy*, 1958, pp. 325-41; K. Baier, "Is Punishment Retributive?", *Analysis*, March, 1955, pp. 25-32; and J. Feinberg, "On Justifying Legal Punishment," *Nomos III, Responsibility*, Carl J. Friedrich, ed., New York, 1960, pp. 152-167.

10. The similarity to Russell's *indefinite descriptions* should be obvious. I do not think that indefinite descriptions will do for my purpose, though, since an indefinite description may not, in practice, be anonymous. The more detailed the description, the more unerring, in context, the identification. ("A blond man standing near the fireplace and wearing a red corduroy shirt"). The anonymous descriptions in question refer to persons only as violators of rules.

CHAPTER IV

THE CHANCELLOR'S FOOT

There are no definite guides for the Judge. He follows his sense of justice, which, like the proverbial Chancellor's foot, varies from Judge to Judge. The sentence in the particular case lies practically uncontrolled in the understanding and conscience of the Judge, and the criteria are vague and almost nonexistent.

S. E. SOBELOFF, "The Sentence of the Court"

To place the debate about punishment is not to resolve it; it is to make it more intelligible, and hence more amenable to reasoned decision. If we have no idea of the context within which punishment is questioned, we have no idea what might count as an answer.

In this chapter we will examine some kinds of disputes which arise over punishment in court: not all. We will not examine such potentially interesting questions as the rationale for setting of bail, for instructions given juries, or for probation and parole. Rather, we shall confine ourselves to the rationale of the determination of guilt, and of sentencing. Our interest will be in exploring the extent to which retributivist and utilitarian theses can be maintained here. This exploration will, we hope, shed some incidental light on judicial reasoning.

Before moving directly to the area of dispute, however, some preliminaries are in order.

I

The first is merely a reminder of the distinction made in Chapter II between descriptive and prescriptive theses. We shall examine the possibilities both that the debate is over the proper

61

description of judicial reasoning, and that it concerns prescriptions for judicial reasoning.

The second preliminary concerns a concept which we have until now used freely, trusting to the reader's intuitive grasp of it; but which becomes more crucial here, and must therefore be scrutinized carefully. It is that of a "consideration." One way, a way we have already used, of putting retributive and utilitarian theses, is to speak of what is and is not a "consideration" in the justification of punishment. This word I have used as a substitute for "acceptable reason." Yet another form of language which could be used to speak of what is and is not "relevant."

Considerations are *prima facie* reasons, but they may have no application in the particular discussion. Thus it is a consideration in discussions in which people justify changing jobs that the salary in the new job is higher; but it may not in a particular case where the salary is the same be a reason. This distinction between reasons and considerations is sometimes overlooked because there is use of "reason" which is equivalent to "consideration" as when it is said that such and such is a good reason in general but that it does not apply in this particular case.

One way to approach the concept "consideration" is to note the factors which limit it: the bounds beyond which we are not willing to call a form of words a consideration. Of these we may list briefly five, without of course claiming exhaustiveness for our list.

First, it should be clear that there are certain forms of words which could only in the most unusual circumstances if at all operate as considerations. "Ouch! my leg!," "I now pronounce you man and wife," "Where is the salt?," seem unlikely ever to qualify as considerations. No doubt there are many forms of words about which it would be difficult to decide whether they could function as considerations, especially if the context of the discussion in which they are nominated as considerations is not specified; but this does not destroy the point that there are forms of language not generally eligible to serve as considerations.

Secondly, considerations have to do with the grounds for decisions rather than the causes of them. If the umpire remarks, after announcing that the runner is safe, that he thinks his words were the result of post-hypnotic suggestion, then he is not offering a consideration in support of his decision. Neither is a judge backing his sentence by a reason if he remarks, after passing sentence, "I have a very severe headache, and whenever I have a severe headache I find myself favoring execution rather than life imprisonment."

Third, if a statement is a consideration in one case, then it is a consideration in every similar case. To say, "C is a consideration in case A but not in case B, even though case B is similar in every relevant respect to case A" is to speak nonsense. It is not open to us, for example, to claim that increase in salary is a consideration for Jones, who has been offered a new position, but not for Smith, who has been offered one too—unless we are prepared to point to a relevant difference in the circumstances surrounding the offer to Smith. If it is not a consideration for Smith, everything else being equal, it was not a consideration for Jones.

Fourth, to say that C is a consideration in a certain *sort* of discussion is to say that, everything else being equal, it is conclusive. Here "everything else being equal" has the force of "everything is as might be expected," or "no special explanation applies." Increase in salary is a consideration in discussions of new positions, but may not be a reason for Smith if he is independently wealthy, or has taken a poverty vow, or expects the value of the currency to collapse. But if everything else *is* equal, then to show that salary would be higher would be to show that Smith should take the position.

Fifth, the range of considerations relevant to a certain sort of discussions varies with the importance of arriving at agreement in discussions of that sort: the smaller the importance the greater the range. We do not attach much importance to the choice of neckties, so we are willing to accept "I just like blue," or even, "My guardian angel says take that one" as considerations. There is almost no end to the line of reasons a man could give for choosing a given necktie; but there is an end to the line of reasons a judge can give as ground for death sentence rather than life imprisonment. What his guardian angel tells him is not a consideration unless a special theological or sociological explanation is forthcoming.

Very much more would have to be said in anything like a complete analysis of this difficult concept. This may be enough for our immediate purposes. Let us now turn to the question what *retributive* and *utilitarian* considerations are. For our purposes, we will posit that *retributive considerations* are considerations which tend to show that a person or crime deserves punishment, or a given mode and measure of punishment. Retributive considerations are often "backward-looking": having to do with what was done by the defendant. But this need not be so, for retributive considerations can also be used hypothetically ("If a man should kidnap a child, he would deserve death" in legislative discussion; or to refer to contemporaneous events ("He deserves a court-martial for this."—said as the Corporal sleeps at his post). *Utilitarian considerations,* though typically "forward-looking" are, for similar reasons, not necessarily so. They are better defined as considerations which tend to show that to punish a person, or set a penalty on a crime, would have good consequences on the whole. Bentham and the English Utilitarians would, of course, interpret "good consequences" as the minimization of mischief, or the promotion of public happiness. The prevention of crime would be a special case of minimizing mischief, which would in turn be a special case of promoting the public happiness. As we shall see, it is often not easy to practice to decide whether a given consideration is utilitarian or retributive.

Yet one more preliminary piece of road-clearing must be done. Until now we have also left to the reader's intuitive understanding the concept of "justification." This has been excusable, if at all, on the ground that an analysis was not yet crucial, in that it would merely have pointed up an additional source of obscurity in the traditional debate. But now we must deal with a debate between judicial retributivists and utilitarians over what it is that *justifies* the infliction of punishment, or the infliction of it in a given manner and degree. So, beyond speaking of considerations and their interplay, we must say something about the kind of activity within which these considerations are used.

Justification consists in the giving of reasons why an action (course of action, rule, principle, policy, institution) should be regarded as right (desirable, appropriate, preferable, beneficial) in the circumstances. This giving of reasons in favor *of* something is always *to* someone, and *against* something else.[1] The importance of the direction of justification we have already stressed in our discussion of the traditional retributivist position. There is nothing necessarily "relativistic" in the notion that we should look for the addressee (or addressees) of justification. One party's interest in the course of action, policy, etc. may simply be different from another party's; so that what is pertinent here, may be irrelevant there. If the F. B. I. wants to know what I am doing walking about a secret installation without a permit, it will not do (as it would in other circumstances) to say that I make it a principle to walk two miles each day for my health. This is but a facet of the familiar, and I believe, correct, notion that there is no single sufficient description of an action: What is from one point of view potential sabotage, is from another point of view daily exercise, from another an indication of neurosis, from another an illustration of the laws of motion, from another a threat to wild game, and so on. There is no end to the standpoints from which objections can arise; and the point of keeping in mind the direction of justification of punishment is that we are not so likely to think that there is a single sufficient justification; and are more likely to keep our justification pertinent to actual or possible objections from given standpoints.

Justification is, in general, then, simply the answering of objections actually arising or likely to arise. But it is not justification in general that concerns us here, but moral justification. Can an action, policy, or practice be *completely* justified on moral grounds? The answer might seem to be Yes, because, it might be held, moral objections all arise from the moral standpoint and to answer all such objections is to square the act with anyone looking at it from that standpoint. But this is a deceptively metaphorical way of talking. There is no one moral standpoint, and moral objections are of different and potentially conflicting sorts, and are settled by appeal to different and potentially conflicting criteria. There can be moral objections on the grounds of infringement of moral rights, failure to abide by moral duty, injustice, inhumanity, lack of respect for moral obligations, or lack of concern for the common good. And what seems just, or for the common good, or humane by one criterion, might not seem so according to another. Moral justification can be complete only in the sense that the sorts of objections likely to arise have been satisfactorily answered. Where there are potentially conflicting criteria of moral rightness or goodness, there is not always actual conflict. What the utilitarian regards as meeting his criterion may be held by the retributivist to meet his as well. But this kind of "completeness" is in a sense fortuitous, depending on the contingent absence of conflicts of judgment concerning the matter at issue. I do not claim to know an abstract general formula by which a justification may be warranted as complete.

That justification is always *against* something else follows from the kind of role that justification plays in discourse. It would not make sense to require of a man that he justify his behavior if we knew that he had no choice but to behave as he did. We do not ask parachutists to justify their moving downward rather than upward, asthmatics to justify their gasping, coaches to justify substituting only members of the team, or pilots to justify (eventually) landing. But if there is a choice, then there is room for the demand for justification to arise. For then it could seem that what the agent chose to do was not what he ought to have chosen. If the parachutist chose to jump (was not just shoved out) the question can arise whether he ought to have jumped. This brings us to the next point.

Justification is of an action (policy, rule, principle, institution) which if not *prima facie* wrong, or less desirable than some alternative, is at least not clearly better. Ordinarily I do not have to justify driving on the right-hand side of the road, in the United States; nor being married to but one woman; nor placing stamps on my letters. Justifications meet likely or actual objections; and if the action, policy, etc. is *prima facie* wrong; we can know in advance what those objections are likely to be. It is here, perhaps, that the illusion of a complete or sufficient justification arises.

Justification must, as Austin warned us, be kept distinct from excuse. The difference is that in justifying my decision I do not admit that what I decided to do was wrong, but attempt to show that it was right ("It was to prevent his throwing the lamp that I killed him."); in giving an excuse I admit that it was, in general, wrong, but claim that I am not to blame because of some exonerating circumstance. ("I was insane when I killed him.")

Finally we must bring on stage what, for ease of exposition, we have kept so far in the wings; the difference between the justification of acts, and of other things. Specifically, we will be interested in the difference between the justification of judicial decision, of legal rules, and of the institution of punishment.[2] That there is a difference is of course crucial for the argument of this book. Were it not so, there would be nothing wrong with that dissecting-table approach to "the" justification of punishment which we have rejected. We will not here argue that there are differences between the judge's and legislator's, and reformer's problems in justifying punishment; but will in this and the following chapters simply try to make out what it is.

II

Our plan of action, these preliminaries out of the way, is to explore the utilitarian-retributivist controversy as it applies, or can be made to apply, to two different sorts of judicial decision: the finding of guilt and the sentence. The two positions will be examined both as descriptive and as prescriptive theses, to the effect that *only* retributive or *only* utilitarian considerations count in the justification, in judicial contexts, of the infliction, or of the mode and measure, of punishment.

Contemporary retributivists have generally assumed that if there is anywhere they are on strong ground it is at the level of the determination of guilt. Here, surely, the judge must appeal to retributive considerations alone, and exclude utilitarian ones! Yet the matter is not so simple as it seems.

The question whether a person should be punished at all can arise in circumstances in which the crime of which he is accused does or does not bear mandatory legal consequences.

If there are mandatory legal consequences, then to find the defendant guilty is, by the same token, to find him liable to suffer at least the minimal consequences set by law. The question here reduces to the considerations to which the judge could appeal in support of his finding of guilt. This is in turn reduced to the questions what the accused did, and whether what he did constitutes violation of the law. Considerations to which the judge appeals may bear on either of these issues. That the judge looks back to what was done is not sufficient evidence that the judge makes use only of retributive considerations; for it must be shown that his concern in looking back is solely with what the accused deserves.

Suppose that there is a mandatory minimum sentence of five years' imprisonment for manslaughter, and the defendant, a medical practitioner, is accused of manslaughter on grounds of criminal negligence: he prescribed that a patient should be wrapped in flannels soaked in kerosene for three days, and as a result of this treatment she died.[3] Several questions must be distinguished: *Descriptive Questions:* (1) May the judge appeal solely to retributive considerations in determining guilt? (2) May the judge appeal solely to utilitarian considerations? (3) May he appeal to retributive considerations at all? (4) May he appeal to utilitarian considerations at all? *Prescriptive Questions:* (1) Should the judge appeal solely to retributive considerations? (2) Should the judge appeal solely to utilitarian considerations? (3) Should he appeal to retributive considerations at all? (4) Should he appeal to utilitarian considerations at all?

The considerations of which the judge may make use are, first of all, factual ones: the defendant did or did not do this and that (prescribe what it is claimed he prescribed). They are also causal: the doing of this and that had certain consequences (the prescription was the cause of the death). And they are legal, having to do with the question whether the doing of this and that, which caused so and so, constitutes criminal negligence. It could be, and has been, *argued* that all of these questions are in the last analysis factual ones: concern empirical and legal fact. If this is correct, then it does not immediately follow that the judge is concerned with what the defendant *deserves,* and that the "factual" considerations are really retributive in that they tend to support the conclusion that the defendant deserves five years' imprisonment.

It could also be, and has been, *argued* that what appears to be merely factual inquiry is not so. For the question[4] whether what the defendant did constitutes criminal negligence turns on the question whether what he did would be reckless in a man of "ordinary prudence." But this decision, it has been argued, is —or at least involves—a decision of "policy." The judge is, and must recognize that he is, setting a precedent. What are the advantages and disadvantages of declaring that a man of "ordinary prudence" would or would not act as this medical practitioner acted?

Is the judge discovering the law or creating it, in handing down his decisions? If the former, then the rationale of his decision need have nothing to do with desert; if the latter, then it is open to him to take into account the well-being of everyone concerned in setting his precedent. He is indeed a legislator:

"Nay whoever hath an absolute authority to interpret any written or spoken laws, it is he who is the lawgiver to all intents and purposes, and not the person who first wrote or spake them."[5] But if the judge is, in interpreting, creating law, then whatever considerations bear on what the law ought to be, bear by the same token on the interpretation of it. So that if this view is taken, and if, as we shall find, and no one doubts, utilitarian considerations enter into legislation, to that extent they enter into judicial decision of guilt.

We are not likely, and will not attempt, to settle this debate in legal philosophy here. It is sufficient for our purpose if we have shown that, descriptively speaking, it is not open to us simply to agree that the considerations to which the judge appeals are retributive only. It is not clear even that they are retributive at all; since they may be merely "factual;" and it is not clear that in the determination of the "facts," the judge may exclude considerations of "policy." Neither retributive nor utilitarian considerations can be ruled out on the ground that the judge may not appeal to them.

Suppose that the accused is found guilty of violating a given law, but that there is no mandatory minimum legal consequence. Then the same considerations which bear on the justification of the sentence will bear on the justification of sentencing. If we can rule out all but one or the other kind of consideration in the justification of mode and measure, we should be able to do the same for the determination whether to punish at all. For on one thesis the mode and measure will turn on degree of desert, and on the other it will turn on the degree of the public need for prevention of mischief; and determination whether to punish becomes determination whether the lowest permissible degree of punishment will serve retribution or prevention. This leads us to an examination of the considerations which bear on the sentence awarded.

III

As will be noted from the quotation with which I began this chapter, the considerations to which the judge appeals cannot be assumed to be very clear and precise. Any attempt to make them this way will be an attempt to introduce precision where it is not found "in nature." Nevertheless, we are fortunate in finding that in England a beginning has been made. Here, what counts as a consideration for or against a sentence is crystallized out much more sharply than in the United States. In England it is possible to appeal the sentence separately from the verdict of "guilty," though in the United States it is not possible to do this.[6] Therefore, since sentences may in England be reviewed and criticized, the considerations which may be taken into account by the judge in sentencing are much more explicitly mentioned in legal literature. There the sentence may be appealed if the judge, in sentencing, has "proceeded upon wrong principles." Some of these principles are spelled out quite explicitly in *Halsbury's Laws of England*.[7]

> The court, in fixing the punishment for any particular crime, will take into consideration (1) the nature of the offense and the circumstances in which it was committed, (2) the degree of deliberation shown by the offender, (3) the provocation which he has received, if the crime is one of violence, (4) the antecedents of the prisoner up to the time of his sentence, his age and character, and any recommendations to mercy which the jury may have made.

> Moreover among the factors which may be considered are (5) particular circumstances such as the prevalence of a particular offense, or (6) the abuse of a position in a public service, or (7) the need to keep secure a particular public service, or (8) that by nature of the legislation creating the offense it is apparent that heavy pecuniary penalties may be required.

> (9) It is the practice of criminal courts generally to punish persistent offenders more severely than those who have not been previously convicted or have not committed other crimes, but (10) it is not right to be guided merely by previous convictions, and (11) it is a well recognized principle that a severe sentence for a trifling offense cannot be justified merely on the ground that the offender has had many previous convictions. On the other hand, (12) a first offender may commit an offense of such malignity that a severe sentence is properly imposed. (13) Previous conviction in another country may be taken into consideration in passing sentence. (14) An unnecessarily long period of detention before a trial is a matter to be considered in passing sentence.

> (15) There is no rule of law or practice that a prisoner who has given evidence for the Crown against a fellow prisoner should receive a lighter sentence in view of this.

This list could no doubt be tremendously extended if less general principles were mentioned; and it might be held that the list could be reduced to three or four principles which can serve as the reason for all the others. I would of course be willing to include any considerations of the same level of generality which might have been left out in Halsbury. This is not intended as a "complete" list; but it could be indefinitely long if we were to accept less and less general considerations.[8] If the list must be reduced, I would not want to do it in such a way as to distort judicial reasoning. I would have no objection to saying that some of these considerations are "included in" others, or that they are the "foundation" or "ground" of others. No doubt, when some of these considerations are challenged, other more general ones are appealed to for support. For example, when the question is raised why a more severe sentence should be awarded if the crime involves abuse of a position in public service, it could be answered that severe punishment may be necessary to deter other public servants from similar crimes, and that if public servants are not deterred from taking advantage of their positions, an undesirable state of affairs will arise, and that we ought to do what we can to avoid undesirable states of affairs. But most such "subsumptions" hide more than they reveal about the nature of justification.

Can the judicial retributivist or utilitarian make out a convincing case for the descriptive thesis that judges, in awarding sentence, are confined to retributive or to utilitarian considerations? Two difficulties become apparent. First, there are considerations (I will christen them "Janus-considerations") which seem to point both toward desert and toward prevention or other desired consequences. Secondly, even where a consideration seems to qualify, *prima facie*, as utilitarian or retributive, it can hardly be ruled out as relevant by the party whose interest lies in the other direction.

1.) Note consideration no. 15 in Halsbury's list. Does it look toward prevention or desert? It says that the fact that a criminal has assisted the court by informing on a fellow-defendant does not exonerate him in any degree for his crime. It also says that the consequences of paying off a criminal in this way, by reducing his sentence, are not likely to be desirable. The 10th and 11th principles seem also to have this Janus-effect. Ten says *either* that it is unjust to an offender to measure out punishment strictly in accordance with previous offenses, since other factors may tend to exonerate; *or* that it is unwise to take only previous convictions into account in deciding punishment, since recidivists would have no reason to choose the lesser of two crimes where "crimes compete."

2.) Take now some considerations which seem *prima facie* to be clearly retributive or utilitarian. The first, 2nd, 3rd, 4th, 13th, and 14th, seem retributive; the 5th, 6th, and 7th utilitarian. Take the 2nd. This seems clearly retributive, because a man deserves more punishment as his crime was done with a greater degree of deliberation. But may the utilitarian judge be oblivious to the degree of deliberation? Is there no utilitarian advantage in awarding a lighter sentence to crime done "in the heat of passion" than to cold and calculated crime? Will not increasing the penalty for calculated crime be likely to impress the potential calculating criminal? But—from the standpoint of the utilitarian—is there any value in awarding heavy penalties for crimes of passion, which by definition allow no time to think? To be precise, there are two ways in which the utilitarian judge is concerned with the degree of deliberation. 1) Because (sometimes) he wants to deter the criminal from future calculated crime by adding the likelihood of punishment as a factor to be taken into calculation; 2) Because (more frequently) he wants to deter other potential calculating criminals by the example of the fate of this one.

It would seem that the closer we look at the matter the more principles listed in Halsbury tend to degenerate into Janus-principles. A man deserves less punishment (3) if he has received great provocation; but there is good utilitarian reason for punishing him less, since part of the mischief in the case was the provocation itself, which must be discouraged. A regard to the "antecedents" (4) good or bad of the criminal, can be justified on the ground that punishing criminals with bad antecedents more severely can have desirable deterrent effects; as well as on the more obvious ground that the desert of a man with bad antecedents is worse than that of a man with good.

To whatever extent it is impossible to say of a given consideration that is utilitarian or retributive, it is impossible to maintain that the way in which judges use this consideration supports the descriptive utilitarian or retributivist thesis; and the less intelligible the prescriptive theses become, according to which only one or the other kind of consideration should be appealed to by judges in the justification of sentences.

Could it be that *any* consideration to which the judge appeals could be retributive, given the proper interpretation; and any could be utilitarian? Then does the controversy collapse, and the combatants go home to lick their wounds? This would be a happy outcome; but it is, unfortunately, too easy. We cannot with our Janus-considerations wipe out the difference between a retributivist and a utilitarian judge. They may chance upon the same considerations, but they pick up and wield them for different reasons. And it is the reason for which they are wielded that makes them retributive or utilitarian; not some internal mark. For they must *tend to show* that the criminal deserves his sentence, or that good consequences are likely to follow from it. But since many, if not all, considerations on Halsbury's list can be made to point in *either* direction, the thesis that only retributivist (or only utilitarian) considerations are relevant in the justification of sentences is not so restrictive as it seemed.

But what of the descriptive theses? Since I have no good reason to suppose that the judge may point Halsbury's considerations in only one direction, I have no reason for accepting either descriptive utilitarianism or retributivism with respect to the rationale of sentences. To say that only e.g. retributive considerations are relevant in the justification of sentences may now be understood as saying that there are no persons who may properly be called judges who use these very same considerations for another purpose. And this is, as we have seen, absurd.

Let us turn now to the prescriptive theses. *Should* judges reason on solely retributivist, or solely utilitarian grounds, in justifying their sentences?

Perhaps the best way to understand the utilitarian and retributive views here is to see them as alternative proposals concerning the part the judge should play in the system. The utilitarian would presumably hold that the judge's business within the defined limits of his discretion is, roughly, to sentence in such a way that the best results possible in the circumstances will be produced. The judge becomes on this view a sort of "social engineer," who, working with the tools given him by the legislators, accomplishes as much good as he can in the particular case with which he has to deal. He is limited so far as his equipment goes to terms in jail and fines; but he can clearly do a better or a worse job of rehabilitation or deterrence in the circumstances. He should make full use of the aid and advice of psychiatrists and social workers so that he can take full advantage within his limitations, (he can only assign a sentence between five and twenty years, for example) of the opportunity before him to maximize the social good.

The retributivist, on the other hand, would think of the judge not as a queer sort of social worker but as the stern balancer of the scales of justice. On this view it is the business of the judge to see to it that the prisoner gets no more or no less than is due him because of the seriousness of the crime. Here to think of the judge as a social engineer is impertinent and even dangerous. It is impertinent because the working of justice would be interfered with by a kind of amoral opportunism: a taking advantage of the immediate situation to promote good in any way possible within the rules. It is dangerous because justice in this society is imperiled if each convicted criminal is considered simply as a pawn to be used in the great enterprise of social improvement. There will have been substituted for the attempt to do what is absolutely right by the criminal, the attempt to do with the criminal whatever will serve the interest of the whole.

Now as we have seen, so far as the Anglo-American legal system is concerned, we cannot find a clear picture of either the Social Engineer or the Stern Balancer. The rules do not exclude considerations appropriate to either. We have quoted Halsbury for considerations typically taken into account in England. Sobeloff mentions, among other things, that the American judge in deciding sentence takes into consideration the protection of society, retribution against the criminal, the nature of the crime, the personality of the criminal, the question of how the man can best be treated, and the legitimate expectation of the public that its sense of justice will not be offended.

Which type of consideration (so far as we can classify them as retributive or utilitarian) should *predominate* then in the deliberations of the judge? How can we possibly answer this question? One way to approach it is to consider what conditions are likely to favor the conception of the judge as Stern Balancer, and which as Social Engineer.

The Balancer is favored if most of the crimes he tries are of the sort that are also torts: that is, crimes which injure specifiable persons or damage their property.[9] This is not to say that under certain circumstances criminal cases should be handled like civil ones where the defendant is made directly responsible to the person he has injured[10] but that the element of responsibility to the other party cannot be entirely ignored in passing sentence. The sentence may legitimately be criticized in such cases as failing to provide adequate redress for the injury. Here we have specific parties, and clear cases of imbalance between them. If the judge pays no attention to the manner in which punishment is made to balance out against injury, he is to that extent a bad judge.

But the sorts of considerations to which the judge appeals in balancing punishment against injury are retributive. That is, he will refer to what the man has done to his victim. The judge will do this to show that what "the law" is doing to the defendant is *in proportion* (only just, equitable).

While the paradigms of crime will on this view be crimes which are also torts, this conception of punishment may by analogy be extended to crimes such as smuggling and robbing the mails. Here the profit of the crime accrues to the criminal at the expense of the people as a whole. The criminal has enriched himself unjustly by taking a share of the public's goods, or by refusing to contribute to the public coffers his due share. By yet another extension treason and perjury may be brought under the "balancing" concept. Treason is like failing to keep faith with the organization of which one is a member or the company for which one works, thus tending to bring about the destruction or failure of these groups. Justice is thrown out of balance if the perpetrator of such consequences is allowed to have the advantage of his crime unmolested. The perjurer reaps unfair advantage for self or friends by perverting the very process of legal inquiry to his own ends. It is just that such a man, who damages what is of value to the community, should himself go unscathed.

Crime is sometimes distinguished from torts on the basis that the former is against the state, whereas the latter is against individuals only. While this is no longer very widely accepted as an accurate definition; it is easy to see in the light of the preceding analysis, what its appeal is. In torts, an arbitrator is provided to see that justice is done between private parties. Where it is felt that damage done concerns all of the people as well as the ones injured, then we have crime. And here the right which individuals have to recompense or reparation becomes the right of the court to exact whatever is necessary to balance the account with the people.

One final factor remains to be mentioned in the conception of the judge as Balancer of the Scales. The scales must be balanced not only between criminal and victim or society, but also between criminal and criminal. Indeed it is here that the conception seems most solidly grounded. For if the scale by which the criminal and his victim or society is weighed be rejected as a fiction; it seems harder to reject the scale by which the treatment of criminal A for crime C is weighed against the treatment of criminal B for crime C. Considerations which, couched in the language of "desert," tend to show that this kind of balance has been achieved, are hard to exclude from the judge's vocabulary.

The conception of the judge as Social Engineer is favored under other circumstances: (1) If it is evident that the persons coming before the court can by careful handling be discouraged from repeating their crimes (a special court for recidivists, for drug addicts, or for alcoholics is conceivable: though, of course, the need for careful handling is not limited to special courts). (2) If the law makes parents, employers, or teachers of a defendant responsible for changing conditions which "cause" his law-breaking. (3) If the judge has a monopoly on certain means to social improvement (committing offenders to reformatories, state hospitals, etc.). (4) If the society is unstable and lacks homogeneity. In such a situation the wise man is more useful than any tightly drawn set of rules made out by a legislature. Here the social good the judge can accomplish is vastly greater if he is not reduced to the position of a rule-interpreting "bureaucrat."

Under such circumstances we easily come to think of the judge as an official in a system which has a clear purpose.[11] The system includes, besides judges, policemen, guards, detectives, constables, sheriffs, posses and wardens. The purpose of the system is to reduce crime.[12] But since the means which the judge must use are in themselves socially undesirable because they involve pain and inconvenience, he must use them as sparingly as possible and may frequently be called upon to account for their use. That is to say, a justification may be demanded for the sentence he has pronounced.[13] The sort of justification the judge offers is analogous to the explanation the city manager offers when the water must be cut off for a day; or that the road department offers for closing off an important artery for a month; or that the contractor gives us when he insists that expensive concrete piers must be put down to bedrock. The judge is telling us how what seems on the face of it undesirable must be tolerated if certain evil consequences are to be avoided, that is if crime is to be reduced and not to increase. Just as the city manager tells us we must make do without water for a day if the water tank is to be repaired and serious leaks plugged; so the judge tells us that if we expect to reform the juvenile before the court, he must be taken in hand for a period of time by the law and suffer the inconvenience and shame of a stay in the Reformatory. If an irate citizen calls the city manager to complain about the water being cut off the city manager will be more likely to offer forward-looking ("utilitarian") considerations than backward-looking ("retributive") ones. What is to be shown is *what good* will result if the inconvenience is tolerated; not the history of the leaks, the name of the tank manufacturer, etc.: though these details may be used to amplify and support the reasons for the water stoppage. Similarly, if a moralist charges the Juvenile Court judge with indiscriminate or careless infliction of misery, the judge must show what good he expects to do by the sentence. But, to show this it may be useful to offer an analysis of the character and record of the juvenile and of the nature of the crime. Thus, even though the justification of sentences by the judge considered as Social Worker may be utilitarian in essence; this still does not rule out retributive considerations.[14]

The point about the differing conceptions of the judge is that of course the conditions which favor *either* role the judge may play or both of them are likely to be present, so we can find no ground for ruling out one role or the other. The judge in fact has more than one purpose in passing down his sentences. He must be continually weighing these purposes against each other. It is not possible to weigh once in advance and have done with it. If there were not multiple purposes which the player of the role must serve, then we might conceivably put experts of this or that variety into it. Criminologists (to whatever extent this field is a science) would be best fitted to determine disposition of criminals, were reform the only purpose. The expertness of the judge (the extent to which he is or is not an expert) could then be sensibly discussed. But as things are, though there are areas in which the expertness of the judge may be discussed (expertness in knowledge of the law in a given field, or in instructing juries); we do not assess judges *qua* judge as more or less expert. We do of course claim that one judge is better than another and in support of such claims we refer to experience, equable temperament, carefulness, intelligence, and so on. But if the sole purpose of the judge were to reduce crime then it surely ought to be legitimate to speak of more or less expert judges.

Would there, under any conceivable circumstances, be ground for *excluding* utilitarian or retributive reasoning on the part of the judge? To agree that there would is to accept the position that there could be circumstances in which judges need not be concerned with the justice, or need not be concerned with the consequences of their sentences. There seems to be no good reason for excluding either concern.

It is difficult to imagine what the proposed practices would be like, whether we are willing to call them "punishment" or not. The circumstances and purposes would certainly be radically different from the circumstances and purposes of punishment. That there are situations in which one would be likely to hear none but utilitarian considerations in court is beside the point. The prescriptions call for a rule of relevance, the acceptance of which would make it at least doubtful whether we should call the officials who must accept these rules *judges* at all.

IV

To sum up: *Descriptive* judicial retributivism and utilitarianism were examined as they applied to the justification of punishing (at all), and as they applied to the sentence. Whether utilitarian considerations are excluded from the judicial justification of punishing is debatable, turning on the acceptance of the thesis that the law is discovered, or of the thesis that it is at least partially created by the judge. Retributive considerations may play a part in the justification of punishing where minimal legal consequences are not mandatory, but so may utilitarian consequences. Neither utilitarian nor retributivist consequences may be excluded from the justification of sentences. *Prescriptive* judicial retributivism or utilitarianism were found to be acceptable to the degree that conditions favor the conception of the judge as Balancer or as Social Engineer, respectively. But since conditions can change, neither prescription can be accepted without qualification. No satisfactory ground was found for *excluding* either conception of the judge, no matter what the circumstances.

CHAPTER IV

FOOTNOTES

1. Cf. Joel Feinberg, "On Justifying Legal Punishment," *Nomos* III, *Responsibility*, C. J. Friedrich, ed., New York 1960, pp. 152-67.
2. Unnecessary theoretical confusion is engendered if we set up a schematic abstract relationship between act, rule, and practice. I prefer to bypass this by avoiding the general account and moving directly to the more specific one.
3. Commonwealth v. Pierce (Supreme Judicial Court of Massachusetts, 1884) 138 Mass, 165, 52 Am. Rep. 264.
4. To say nothing of the disputes over the "policy" element in causal questions in the law. Cf. e.g., H. L. A. Hart and A. M. Honore, "Causation in The Law," *Law Quarterly Review*, LXXII (1956), Pt. I, pp. 58-90; reprinted in H. Morris, ed., *Freedom and Responsibility*, Stanford, California, 1961.
5. Bishop Hoadley, as quoted in H. L. A. Hart, *The Concept of Law*, Oxford, 1961, p. 137.
6. S. E. Sobeloff, "The Sentence of the Court," an address delivered before the Criminal Law Section of the American Bar Association, Chicago, August 16, 1954. (Mimeographed copy in possession of Professor M. Curtis, Cornell Law School).
7. Third Edition, Vol. 10, pp. 488-89, (numerals mine). Each of these points is supported in Halsbury by reference to leading cases.
8. For example, in R. V. O'Connell (1909), 73 J. P. 118; Cr. App. Rep. 11, C.C.A. the sentence of the judge in a manslaughter case was reduced from ten to three years because "they thought the judge who had tried the case had allowed two circumstances to weigh with him too much—(1) the fact that the appt. did not give the deceased man a chance of 'putting up his hands' (2) that it made no difference to the offense whether the body of the deceased man was in a 'diseased condition.' This is said to show that a wrong standard or principle has been applied in the particular case under consideration."
9. According to a popular legal textbook (William L. Prosser, *Hand Book of the Law of Torts*, St. Paul, Minnesota, 1941), a tort is "a term applied to a miscellaneous and more or less unconnected group of civil wrongs, other than breach of contract, for which a court of law will afford a remedy in the form of an action for damages. The law of torts is concerned with the compensation of losses suffered by private individuals in their legally protected interests, through conduct of others which is regarded as socially unreasonable." (Page 1). Prosser distinguishes between torts and crimes as follows: "A tort action is brought by the injured party to cover compensation for the damage he has suffered. Criminal proceedings are brought by the State to protect the interests of the public against the wrong-doer. The same act may be, although it is not necessarily, both a tort against an individual and a crime against the State; and in such a case the wrong-doer may be

subject to both a civil action in tort and a criminal prosecution." (p. 10).
Turner gives us a rule for deciding whether a crime is a tort as follows: "If
we know any particular occurrence to be a crime, it is easy—as we have
seen—to ascertain whether or not it is also a tort, by asking if it damages
any assignable individual. But there is no corresponding test whereby when
we know an occurrence to be a tort, we can readily ascertain whether or
not it is also a crime." (Turner, J. W. C., ed., *Kenny's Outlines of Criminal
Law*, 16th edn., Cambridge, 1952, p. 543.)

10. I do not mean to reject this approach either.

11. That this purpose may become dangerously unclear is indicated by the
following account of justice in France during the time of the galleys: "but
the bulk of the *chiourme* was supplied by the *parlements*, the king's courts
of justice. They were charged with the duty of sending to the galleys those
they condemned. . . . It is certain that if there had been no need of arms to
pull the galley sweeps then the future of the condemned would have been
quite different . . . they . . . had the role of recruiting sergeants. . . . But
they were not always successful; the Intendent of Poitou complained after
a visit to Bellac, where he could only obtain five condemnations to the galleys,
that 'the judges are not really under control.' . . . This very utilitarian view
of punishment did not always suit the taste of the judicial authorities. They
did not hesitate to remind the Intendant that, when all was said and done,
criminals were sent to the galleys as a consequence of their wrong-doing."
Michel Bourdet-Pleville, *Justice in Chains*, London, 1960, pp. 10-13.

12. This is of course an oversimplification. For elaboration, Cf. Bentham, *op. cit.*,
Chapter XIV.

13. "An act of punishment is a choice of something, which, in a sense is an evil,
i.e., the infliction of pain: acts of the order first mentioned have an opposite
character—they are foundations and creations of something good." Aristotle,
Politics, VII, viii, 6-7. ". . . punishment ought not to be inflicted . . . where
it is too *expensive*." Jeremy Bentham, *op. cit.*, XIII, 3.

14. Inspired by his studies in anthropology, Karl Llewellyn published an article
extolling this general view of criminal law and contrasting it to what he calls
the "arms length" conception. On the system he approves, the culprit is
considered as one of the team who has somehow gone wrong, and it is up to
everybody concerned to find out what is wrong, and to get him "back on the
track." On the "arms length" conception the culprit is disposed of according
to the results of a "game" played according to strict rules by two lawyer-
adversaries. (K. N. Llewwellyn, "The Anthropology of Criminal Guilt," in
Social Meaning of Legal Concepts, 2, *Criminal Guilt*, New York University
School of Law, New York, 1950, pp. 100-11.)

Chapter V

LEGAL PENALTIES AND MORAL OFFENSES

Let us follow Nature, who has given shame to man for
his scourge; and let the heaviest part of the punishment
be the infamy attending it. But if there be some countries
where blame is not a consequence of punishment, this
must be owing to tyranny, which has inflicted the same
penalties on villains and honest men.

Montesquieu, *The Spirit of The Laws*

I

Here we turn to some varieties of punishment-justification
which occur in legislative contexts. Our approach will be more
historical than in the previous chapter. Legislative discussion is
more amorphous than judicial. It does not lend itself to classification according to the stage of the proceedings in the way that
judicial discussion does. The legislative debate cannot be an-
alyzed by moving from step to step in the legislative "process."
We must look, rather, to differing conceptions of what the legislator is and is doing. This leads us back to our main theoretical
antagonists, Kant and Bentham. We will deal with both as if they
were speaking to legislative problems. How much justification
there is for treating Kant in this way is hard to know; since, as
we have tried to show, Kant simply did not distinguish carefully
between the different sorts of context punishment-justification
can have. Bentham was speaking most of the time, but not all of
the time, to legislators.[1]

We will not attempt to examine all of the kinds of legislative
punishment-discussion, but only the justifications given for prohibiting and penalizing a given kind of deed, and for penalizing
it in a given manner and degree. And we will omit discussion of
possible descriptive utilitarian and retributive theses, since neither

thesis would be at all plausible: no one, so far as I know, has argued that in fact legislators do not appeal to both retributive and utilitarian considerations. What is more interesting is the recommendation that legislators should confine themselves to one or the other sort of consideration.

Bentham's carefully worked out grounds for the legislative decision whether or not a given deed should be prohibited and penalized have been discussed in the third chapter. There we mentioned the general purpose of maximizing happiness, thus minimizing mischief, and thus of preventing crime; the possible remedies for crime other than punishment; and the circumstances limiting the use of punishment.

In discussing Kantian retributivism in the second chapter, we had more to say about what Kant calls the mode and measure of punishment, than about the grounds on which it is decided that punishment is or is not warranted. The latter question must come first in our approach to a possible legislative retributivism.

It has often been contended against retributivism just that it has no theory of the limits of legal punishment. The retributivist legislator would, presumably, want to prohibit and penalize deeds it would be morally wrong to do. But we have no laws against lying, ingratitude, or lust. Would we want such laws? How do we draw the line here unless we bring in the relative usefulness of the laws? Legislative retributivism breaks down at this point, unless the retributivist is willing to accept the consequence that all that is considered to have moral ill desert should by the same token have legal ill desert.

But that would be the most extreme position. If the retributivist retreats a little from this, there is something much more plausible he may want to say. He may wish to insist that laws ought not to be enacted which penalize morally innocent deeds. And this would be quite another kettle of fish.

Kant, in a passage already quoted, holds that the penalty of death is necessary for murder, since "it is only thus that a sentence can be pronounced over all criminals proportionate to their internal wickedness."[2]

Bradley is, for Bradley, quite explicit.

> What is really true for the moral consciousness; what it clings to, and will not let go; what marks unmistakably, by its absence, a "philosophical" or a "debauched" morality, is the

necessary connection between responsibility and liability to punishment, between punishment and desert, or the finding of guiltiness before the law of the moral tribunal.[3]

Guilt before a "moral tribunal" is apparently here contrasted with guilt before a legal one; and Bradley is saying, that the law ought not to require the punishment of a morally innocent person.

C. W. K. Mundle, a modern retributivist, says "Punishment of a person by the State is morally justifiable if and only if he has done something which is both a legal and a moral offense."[4] It would seem to follow that legislators ought not to pass laws, with penalties attached, which could be violated without committing a moral offense.

Is this a plausible contention, and is it incompatible with legislative utilitarianism? It should first be noted that retributivists need not be understood as saying that the only permissible legal prohibitions are those which penalize what are "in themselves" moral offenses. The distinction between what is a moral offense "in itself" and what is not has been the subject of great confusion, centering around the key terms: *malum in se* and *malum prohibitum*. Bouvier's Law Dictionary defines them as follows:

> An offense *malum in se* is one which is naturally evil as murder, theft and the like; offenses at common law are generally *mala in se*. An offense *malum prohibitum* on the contrary is not naturally an evil, but becomes so in consequence of its being forbidden, as playing in games which, being innocent before, have become unlawful in consequence of being forbidden.[5]

According to Bouvier, Blackstone gives as examples of *mala prohibita*, game laws, laws against exercising certain trades without having served a given apprenticeship. The *mala in se* were held to be binding on conscience, but the *mala prohibita* were not, by Blackstone. *Mala prohibita* are in many legal decisions held to be not "wrong in themselves and apart from positive law," but "merely prohibited by statutes or by common law."

There are obvious difficulties in such a distinction. What is naturally evil and what is evil because a rule has been made against it? How are we to go about answering this question? The distinction seems to suppose it possible to make a separation between what, without any influence from positive law, has always been considered wrong and what has come to be considered wrong, partly or entirely because there has come to be a law against it. But this separation is quite problematic and seems to turn on questions of history which ought to have no place in a philosophical distinction. To make the distinction in this way is to take sides in the discussion between those who hold that there are laws of nature, and those who maintain that the only laws are those found in the statute books. But to make the distinction, it may not be necessary to enter into this hoary dispute.

When we say that something is a moral offense "in itself," we could mean that if a man does it not knowing that it is against the law, he still commits a moral offense. When something is *not* a moral offense, "in itself," then a man can do it not knowing that it is against the law, and *not* have committed a moral offense; although, of course, if he should have known that it was against the law, and had the capacity and opportunity to find out that it was against the law, we would be inclined to say that he had done something morally wrong. Some deeds are moral offenses *not* in themselves, but simply because they are against the law, and there is an obligation to keep the law. What is morally indefensible is to enact and attach a penalty to a law there is no moral obligation to keep.

If this much be granted, then the question is whether the consistent utilitarian would enact such laws. He may well deny that he would. The reason for his denial would be that it is the utilitarian legislator's business to enact laws which maximize happiness and minimize unhappiness. Laws which meet this standard are, then, for the good of everyone alike, and legal penalties are a device used to make them effective. That a law is for the good of everyone alike is ground for saying that there is a moral obligation to abide by it. Indeed, if it does not meet this standard, there is no moral obligation to abide by it; but utilitarians cannot be held liable for laws which they themselves do not approve. Consider a law prohibiting the sale of alcoholic beverages to minors. If the law is justified on utilitarian grounds, to break it is to initiate harmful consequences: to minors, the parents of minors, property owners, employers, and others. None of these particular consequences may follow any particular sale; but any particular sale would risk these consequences. So, to break such a law is a moral offense; and the man who breaks it deserves to be punished. But if the law were not justified on utilitarian grounds, to enact it with penalty attached is to approve what would simply make offenders unhappy, without any compensating gain in happiness for the community.

Now it would seem to follow that there is no ground for dispute between utilitarians and retributivists over the questions which deeds should be penalized in law. But the retributivist need not yet be satisfied. Utilitarians may not only prohibit what would go against the public interest; they may also *require* what promotes the public interest. But we must distinguish between the moral status of acts which are harmful to the public and acts which are not to the public's advantage. We grant that if an act clearly causes damages or injury to specific parties or to the public in general then it is *ipso facto* morally wrong. But should we be as quick to grant the moral wrongness of acts which merely fail to benefit the public? Yet may not such acts be legally required on utilitarian ground? and may not failure to do them be penalized?

It is clearly enough wrong on both utilitarian and retributivist grounds that a person should rob a house: over the penalizing of such a harmful act there is no dispute. But let us suppose for the sake of argument that the welfare of mankind will be *abetted* if everyone can be made to follow certain legal requirements: that he marry only persons approved by the State Genetecist, that he submit to sterilization on order of the State Geneticist, that he contribute one day per week working on the public roads, that he give his pets to an experimental laboratory, that he remain at his present job until he obtains a permit to change. It is over such requirements as these that interesting moral and quasi-moral discussions arise. If it can clearly be shown that positive harm to all will result if one of these regulations is violated, then the retributivists would no doubt agree that to fail to abide by it is a moral transgression. But if it is merely probable that things would be better on the whole were the rule to be followed, then would he agree? Even if it were quite certain that the state of mankind could be improved by rigid genetic control, would there be no moral ground on which to oppose the laws by which that control is imposed?

Is the rift an imaginary or a real one? The utilitarian could contend that it is imaginary. Suppose a program of genetic examination and compulsory sterilization could be shown to hold out great promise of improving the human race in resistance to disease, and physical and mental vigor. Would the utilitarian, any more than the retributivist, immediately set out to enact laws requiring compulsory examination and sterilization of defectives? Only if he was willing to ignore other important values which, together with resistance to disease and physical and mental vigor, go to make up the well-being of the members of the community. It is not even clear, as is often assumed, that the utilitarian view need be so narrow in focus as to exclude a system of rights, legal or moral. For it may be argued that a strictly observed general understanding of the limits beyond which individuals may be imposed upon, for no matter how desirable ends, is for the happiness of everyone concerned. How else, it might be asked, could we assess our rights-observance practices, were it not in terms of the benefits and disadvantages to everyone concerned?

Whether the legislative retributivist would be satisfied with this answer is uncertain. Since he wants, in the name of justice, to insist on the relationship he thinks should exist between punishment and moral desert, he may not be convinced that the sophisticated utilitarian, balancing his values, will always prohibit and penalize the deed that he will.

II

Let us turn now to the opposing views concerning the mode and measure of legal penalties. Bentham's views we have but barely mentioned, in the first chapter; Kant's were there expounded at some length. The purpose of legal punishment, as of the other remedies for crime is, for Bentham, the prevention of crime. But this is, upon closer examination, a complex end. It unfolds into four different *objects* of punishment: (1) ". . . to prevent in as far as it is possible and worth while, all sorts of offences whatsover. . . ." (2) "But if a man needs commit an offence . . . to induce him to commit an offence *less* mischievous . . . of two offences that will either of them suit his purpose." (3) When a man has resolved upon a particular offence, the next object is to dispose him to do *no more* mischief than is *necessary* to his purpose." (4) ". . . whatever the mischief be, which it is proposed to prevent, to prevent it at as *cheap* a rate as possible."[8]

This complex object is best served by following a number of rules, of which we will mention only Bentham's first five.[7] (1) "The value of the punishment must not be less in any case than what is sufficient to outweigh that of the profit of the offence." This would be violated by a law which put a fixed fine, low enough for many to pay, on the crime of murder.[8] (2) "The greater the mischief of the offence, the greater is the expense which it may be worth while to be at, in the way of punishment." This would be violated if we make use of a major penalty (burning alive) for a relatively minor crime (counterfeiting) rather than reserving it for a major crime (incendiarism)[9] (3) "Where two offences come in competition, the punishment for the greater offence must be sufficient to induce a man to prefer the less." A violation would consist in a scale of punishments such that a man would be better off to commit armed robbery than robbery, or treason rather than perjury.[10] (4) "When a man has resolved upon a particular offence, the next object is, to induce him to do no more mischief than what is necessary for his purpose." Violation: if the fine for five blows and five shillings stolen is the same as the fine for ten blows and ten shillings stolen.[11] (5) "The punishment ought in no case to be more than what is necessary to bring it into conformity with the rules here given." This sets the upper limit of punishment, and would be violated by any legal penalty which is not required in that degree by the four-fold object of punishment.

This brief sketch of Bentham's scheme for rational penalty-setting may suffice to warn us away from too-easy "refutations." We will reserve comment, however, until we have had a chance to contrast Bentham's conception of rational legislative penalty-setting with Kant's.

The advantages and shortcomings of Kant's Principle of Equality have already been discussed at some length. A troublesome difficulty, which we have not mentioned, is that Kant claims that his Principle is the *only* principle of just legislation. Why should he claim this? As a matter of fact, people do appeal to maxims of justice which can conflict with the Principle of Equality: for example, to the maxim that it is not just to inflict on a man any more punishment than enough to keep him from repeating the crime and others from imitating him, and the maxim that no one ought to be made to suffer cruel and unusual punishment.[12]

Most people would, I think, be willing to grant that *one* sort of consideration which is relevant in discussions about the justice of a penalty is what might be called the "eye-for-an-eye argument"—(*e.g.* "A man who murders deserves to lose his own life;" "If he goes around breaking legs, let his own legs be broken;" Nobody can complain if he loses an eye because he has destroyed an eye.") But what could Kant's reason be for saying that it is the *only* principle of just legislation? How would Kant defend this contention if we should offer him other generally recognized maxims, such as we have mentioned above, to which people appeal in arguing the justice of legal penalties; and which can conflict with the *lex talionis* in particular cases? We are not willing to believe that Kant was unaware of such maxims.

Does Kant rule out these other maxims on the ground that they refer to the *consequences* of the crime, and thus cannot be a maxim of justice, since justice has nothing to do with consequences? On this ground he might rule out the maxim that it is unjust to inflict on a man any more punishment than enough to keep him from repeating and others from imitating the crime. But if, for the sake of argument, we should agree that such maxims cannot be maxims of justice, justice having nothing to do with consequences, there would remain the possibility of maxims, other than the *lex talionis,* which do not appeal to experience either. The rule that a maxim is not to be taken as relevant, which appeals to consequences, will not suffice—even if accepted—to set off the *lex talionis* from all other possible maxims of justice. We can offer *other* maxims which the legislator can use to derive a penalty, given nothing but a description of the crime.

Suppose that the maxim is not that the culprit shall be made to pay equally for his crime, shall have inflicted on him what he has inflicted on his victim; but that he shall be repaid ten times for the damage he has done his victim. If he removed a man's finger, ten of his shall be removed. We shall call this legislative maxim the "Rule of Ten." What reason does Kant have for preferring the *lex talionis* to the Rule of Ten? On neither of these maxims does the legislator need to appeal to experience.[13]

There is an argument which Kant *could* use, and does seem to hint at, which tends to show that when consequences are ruled out, the only rule by which just penalties can be determined is the *lex talionis*. In the "Addition to the Explanation of the Conceptions of Penal Right," in answering the charge that his principle does not seem to provide a penalty for rape, paederasty, and bestiality, Kant says what he thinks the penalty ought to be according to his principle. And he adds, "These crimes are called unnatural, because they are committed against all that is essential to humanity. To punish them by *arbitrary* penalties, is literally opposed to the conception of a *penal* justice. But even then the criminal cannot complain that wrong is done to him. . . ."[14] The implication is that any penalty *not* in accordance with the Principle of Equality would be arbitrary: that is, there is no ground for choosing anything but what is strictly equal to the crime. Why does Kant imply that the punishment is arbitrary if not equal to the crime?

Suppose we do not make the punishment equal to the crime. Then there must be some definite proportion between punishment and crime. How are we to arrive at this proportion? Is there a better argument for the application of a Rule of Ten than of a Rule of Two or a Rule of Four? (Appeals to consequences are not arguments here.) There seems to be no more reason for choosing one of these ratios than another. If, *e.g.* we make the punishment twice the crime, our decision is simply arbitrary. Why not *ten* times? But the alternative is to adopt the Principle of Equality. There is sufficient reason for adopting this principle, for (1) we must adopt *some* proportion between punishment and crime, (2) either equal or unequal, but (3) there's no more reason for choosing one unequal ratio than another, and we can't choose any unequal ratio without making an arbitrary choice. (4) We don't want to choose a penalty arbitrarily, since this is unjust. (5) We must make the punishment equal to the crime.

This whole argument of course presupposes that consequences should be ruled out, which is what the utilitarian would not grant. No doubt Kant is led to the conception of the Principle of Equality as the only principle of just legislation in another way: from his general justification of punishment as a "hindering of a hindrance of freedom," mentioned in the second chapter. If this is the justification of punishment, then perhaps punishment is justified only to the *extent* that compulsion (crime) is brought to bear in the hindrance of freedom. But to follow this out would lead us to examine obscurities, mentioned in the first chapter, in the notion of punishment as a "hindering of a hindrance of freedom."

III

In spite of the theoretical divergence between legislative utilitarians and retributivists, the convergence in practice (as in judicial decisions) is worthy of our attention. Ignore the partisan arguments starting from an excessively narrow or naïve interpretation of the opposing positions, and you find utilitarian and retributivist legislators agreeing over a vast range of penalties. Like the advocates of the Principle of Equality, Bentham, as we have seen, approves a "greater expense" of punishment, the greater (the mischief of) the offence. He is willing that where the punishment proposed is "of such a nature as to be particularly well calculated to answer the purpose of a moral lesson," it may be stretched "a little beyond that quantity which on other accounts would be strictly necessary."[15] He holds that a punishment should have, ideally, the property of "characteristicalness": whereby there is a real analogy between offence and punishment, which can easily be borne in mind, so that the punishment will not be inefficacious because easily forgotten. And "the mode of punishment, which of all others bears the closest analogy to the offence, is that which in the proper and exact sense of the word is termed *retaliation*." This mode of punishment has, therefore, a great advantage over any other "in the few cases in which it is practicable, and not too expensive."[16]

If we did not know whether a list of penalties had been made out in accordance with the Principle of Equality or with Bentham's rules, would we be able to tell the difference? That we could not tell the difference for any particular list would, of course, not be sufficient reason for either party to abandon his theoretical guns. For it might be merely a contingent matter that this particular list turned out this way; and imporant differences could still crop up in the future. What might some of these differences be? One concerns the relation of penalty to temptation; the other, strict liability.

With reference to his first rule, that the value of the punishment must not in any case be less than what is sufficient to outweigh the profit of the offence, Bentham says:

> The strength of the temptation *ceteris paribus* is as the profit of the offence; the quantum of the punishment must rise with the profit of the offence; *ceteris paribus*, it must therefore rise with the strength of the temptation. This there is no disputing.[17]

In his next sentence, Bentham acknowledges the retributivist's source of worry over this doctrine: "True it is," he says, "that the stronger the temptation the less conclusive is the indication which the act of delinquency affords of the depravity of the offender's disposition."[18] His answer is that where no special depravity on the part of the offender has been shown, or it has been shown that he is of "beneficient disposition," then the temptation he was under ought to be taken into account in reducing the punishment. "But it can never operate so far as to indicate the propriety of making it ineffectual, which it is sure to be when brought below the level of the apparent profit of the offence."[19] This is not a very satisfactory answer to the charge, since it still leaves open the question whether utility is not opposed to justice in the legislative setting of penalties. Here special exonerating circumstances have no place; and the utilitarian legislator must take into account the strength of the general temptation to commit the crime in question. Suppose there is widespread temptation to commit the crime, and good utilitarian reason for suppressing it? Would Bentham not have to say, with Paley, that "The crime must be prevented by some means or other . . . whether they be proportionable to the guilt of the criminal or not?" If great temptation does not excuse, it is a mitigating circumstance; and Bentham has not shown us how to reconcile this with the utilitarian theory of legislation.

There are, as is well known, statutes which have been interpreted as holding a man liable for an act which would not ordinarily be held to be his fault. For example, in *State v. Lindberg* it has been held that where the law prohibited an official of a bank from borrowing from his own bank, and where the defendant borrowed money which he had been assured by another official came from another bank, but which came from his own, the reasonableness of the defendant's mistake was not a defense.[20] Such statutes have been defended on the utilitarian ground that they provide a stronger deterrent to criminal behavior than non-strict-liability statues. Whether such cases provide the ground for an ultimate break between retributivists and utilitarians is not certain. For some utiitarians have argued that the supposed greater deterrent value is not real. And retributivists could argue that there is some degree of fault, *e.g.* in that the defendant did after all choose to enter a profession where this particular strict liability statute was a hazard, and did choose to risk violating it by borrowing money.[21]

This cause for dispute between legislative utilitarians and retributivists is similar to the dispute which arises, but which we did not discuss in the previous chapter, over the judicial doctrine that ignorance of the law is no excuse. This seems to have strong utilitarian but no retributive ground. And for similar reasons it is not certain that we would have here an ultimate breaking-off point between retributivists and utilitarians. There are utilitarian reasons for *opposing* this doctrine; and there are retributive reasons for *accepting* it: though in both cases the reasons on the other side seem stronger. Utilitarians can oppose the doctrine on the ground that it weakens the respect for the law by giving rise to cases which go counter to the public sense of justice; retributivists can contend that the doctrine should be accepted because it is a moral fault in a man that he has not sufficiently studied the laws to which he is subject and (via representation) subscriber.

IV

Legislators as well as judges can be thought of on different models. On one model he is a figure who must tend the scales of justice; must see to it that everyone has his due; to whom the community is a province for the exercise of distributive justice. But the real distributions must take place in the courtroom, so he is at best the handmaiden of the judge. He exists to give the judge the proper legal equipment to balance the scales between legitimate interests and claimants. On the other model, the judge is his "underworker" (Bentham); and he and the judge work together to reduce crime. It is, on this model, up to the legislator (and to the judge in so far as he "concretizes" the law) to decide what acts must be discouraged or encouraged for the public's well-being, and up to the judge to put these prohibitions or requirements into effect.

Kant's conception of the joint responsibility of judge and legislator is brought out in passages in the *Rechtslehre* in which he speaks of the opposite of the state of nature as that of the "civil state . . . as the condition of a society standing under distributive justice,"[22] of the "juridicial state" as "that relation of men to one another which contains the conditions under which it is alone possible for everyone to obtain the Right that is his due,"[23] and of men entering into a civil union in which it is "determined by law what shall be recognized as his" and "secured to him by a competent external power distinct from his own personality."[24]

Bentham's counter-model appears in a passage in which he speaks of the "art of legislation" which "teaches how a multitude of men, composing a community, may be disposed to pursue that course which upon the whole is the most conducive to the happiness of the whole community, by means of motives to be applied by the legislator."[25]

On Kant's model, there is an analogy between penalty paid for crime and price paid for goods. A person cannot make restitution in money or goods for the damage he has done, so he must "pay with his skin." But nobody would want to barter goods if he had to give more than he received. The object of the barter is to get "equal value" of *e.g.*, onions for potatoes: to convince the other side that the potatoes you offer are worth just exactly as much as the onions he has for sale. The judge in a criminal case can be considered as an arbitrator in a case where one party has been damaged and the other demands compensation. He must be able to justify his decision to both parties. He is put in a favorable position for this if the law is based on the *lex talionis*. If the law is based on the Rule of Ten, then the criminal has cause for complaint; and if it is based on the Rule of One-half, the person damaged has cause for complaint. In practice, the judge justifies the sentence to both parties by appeal to the law and its fair application. But to the extent that the judge is a legislator (by setting precedent), he has to justify the law to both parties. Separation of legislators and judges leaves legislators with the job not only of providing penal laws which will work for society's good, but also of providing the judge with a workable balancing scale. The *lex talionis* is a more workable balancing scale for the judge as arbitrator, than a rule which establishes some proportion other than equality between punishment and crime.

To justify a legal penalty is, on this view, to show that it is just. Thus, the legislator is seen as in a quandary. He is responsible for the removal of crime, and is therefore tempted to use legal penalties strictly as a tool for this purpose, without allowing any consideration of justice to the individuals punished to enter into his calculations. But at the same time he recognizes that he really ought to be guided by principles of justice and not only by his own "ulterior" ends. Taking justice as a legislative standard is opposed to taking expediency as the standard. The legislator's choice becomes one of doing what is moral and difficult or immoral and expedient.

But of course legislators, like judges, may be criticized, and may criticize themselves, on both grounds: "expediency" (*i.e.*, the prevention of the mischief of crime and the promotion of desirable ends), and justice (*i.e.*, a defensible relation between what is deserved and what is received for crime). The issue is not between a moral and an immoral way of doing things; but between moral duties: to society at large, and to the individual who commits the crime. One duty is assumed when he takes the vow of office; the other arises whenever in the course of his duty as legislator he must give preference to one class of lawbreakers over another by making the penalty for one crime lighter than the penalty for the other.

One proposed legislator would suffer from a blindness to consequences. (The Goddess of Justice wears a blindfold and carries a balance. The blindfold is to prevent her seeing which individuals are involved; but it also prevents her looking where she is going.) The other suffers from a blindness to justice. (Justice will probably *happen*; but its happening is contigent on its agreeing with utility.) There is no compelling reason why either model should be accepted. Why should the legislator wear blinders either on the side of justice or of utility?

CHAPTER V

FOOTNOTES

1. He intended the theory of punishment elaborated in the *Principles* to apply to judicial contexts as well as legislative ones. He speaks, in the Preface of "the Legislator and his underworkman, the Judge"; and the extended discussion of the individualization of punishment has primarily judicial bearings.
2. *Op. cit.*, p. 198.
3. *Ethical Studies*, London, 1876, p. 4.

4. "Punishment and Desert," *Philosophical Quarterly*, 1954, 216-28, p. 227.
5. 15th ed.
6. *Principles*, p. 289.
7. *Principles*, pp. 290-3. There are thirteen rules in all.
8. *Ibid.*, p. 290, n. 4.
9. *Ibid.*, p. 292, n. 1.
10. My example; Bentham gives none.
11. *Op. cit.*, p. 292, n. 3.
12. A peculiar feature of justice is that while in general what is wanted is that the "scales should be balanced," if the attempt is made to balance them *exactly*, by matching measure for measure the criminal's deed, then the punishment begins to be vengeful and cruel and lose its claim to justice.
13. "He said that for every wrong which they had done to anyone they suffered tenfold; or once in a hundred years—such being reckoned to be the length of man's life, and the penalty thus being paid ten times in a thousand years. If, for example, there were any who had been the cause of many deaths, or had betrayed or enslaved cities or armies, or been guilty of any other evil behavior, for each and all of their offenses they received punishment ten times over, and the rewards and beneficences and justice and holiness were in the same proportion." Plato, *Republic*, X, 615.
14. *Op. cit.*, p. 244.
15. *Op. Cit.*, p. 295 (from Rules 10 and 11).
16. *Ibid.*, pp. 302-3.
17. *Ibid.*, p. 291.
18. *Loc. cit.*
19. *Loc. cit.*
20. 125 Wash. 51, 215 Pac. 41 (1923).
21. For a perceptive discussion on strict liability, *Cf.* Richard Wasserstrom, "Strict Liability in the Criminal Law," *Stanford Law Review*, XII (1960), pp. 730-45; reprinted in Herbert Morris (ed.) *Freedom and Responsibility*, Stanford, 1961, pp. 273-281.
22. *Op. cit.*, p. 156.
23. *Ibid.*, p. 155.
24. *Ibid.*, p. 164.
25. *Op. cit.*, p. 423.

CHAPTER VI

TREATMENT VS. PUNISHMENT

'He is a delightful man,' continued the interpreter, 'but he has suffered terribly from' (here there came a long word which I could not quite catch, only it was much longer than kleptomania) 'and has but lately recovered from embezzling a large sum of money under singularly distressing circumstances; but he has quite got over it, and the straighteners say that he has made a really wonderful recovery; you are sure to like him.'

SAMUEL BUTLER, *Erewhon*

In this chapter, we turn to the debate over the institution of legal punishment: to that important segment of the debate which turns around the concept of responsibility. If no one is responsible for his crime, then, it would seem, no one is eligible for punishment—and the institution is not so much abolished or rejected as allowed to wither. An important intellectual ancestor (too little recognized in the literature) of those sociologists and psychiatrists who question the assumption that most men are responsible for their deeds is Robert Owen, the 19th century social reformer.

I

Early in Owen's life, his thesis was made explicit and provided with a rationale, which though often repeated in differing forms, hardly varied from his earliest work to his latest.[1] He must certainly be counted one of the most single-minded men who ever lived.

In an early work, *Essays on the Formation of the Human Character*, there is a vehement passage which we will use as his first statement of the oft-repeated theme:

How much longer shall we continue to allow generation after generation to be taught crime from their infancy, and when so taught, hunt them like beasts in the forests until they are entangled beyond escape in the toils and nets of the law? When, if the circumstances of those unpitied sufferers had been reversed with those who are surrounded with the pomp and dignity of justice, these latter would have been at the bar of the culprit, and the former would have been in the judgment seat.[2]

We should not say that Owen favored the immediate abolition of punishment. He felt that the whole structure of society should be changed so that punishment would no longer be necessary. "When this rational society shall be formed and men individually and generally shall be trained to act in accordance with it, then shall human punishment and rewards cease and cease forever."[3] Punishment is only part of a radically misguided way of life:

It is not then by any partial changes in society that evil can be removed and man made to enjoy a rational and happy existence. The present system with its organization, classification and individual rewards and punishments must be maintained with all its sufferings, miseries, contests, degradations, endless turmoil and confusion; or it must be altogether abandoned to make room for a new system, true in principle and beneficial in practice.[4]

What are Owen's grounds for demanding this radical change? Owen believes that:

The religious, moral, political and commercial arrangements of society throughout the world have been based from the commencement of history upon an error respecting the nature of man: an error so grievous in its consequences that it has deranged all the proceedings of society, made man . . . perhaps more miserable, than any other animal.[5]

What then, is this error? It is the notion that "man forms his own character." From the earliest ages, it has been the practice of the world to act on the supposition that each individual forms his own character and that, therefore, he is accountable for all his sentiments and habits and consequently merits reward for some and punishment for others."[6]

The principle on which Owen would found all social arrangements is that man's character is formed not by, but for him. *". . . his whole character physical, mental and moral is formed independently of himself."*[7]

One thing Owen means to say by this is that a given person has no choice about the place and circumstances of his birth, nor about the feelings and convictions which are made a part of his nature by training.[8] Another is that the child is originally "characterless" and can be molded in a great variety of ways by circumstances of training.[9] Owen draws from his principle a number of consequences for educational, legal, political, and economic reform. For our purpose, the most important is that nobody ought to be punished. The argument that nobody ought to be punished is, when fully made out, as follows.

(1) Every man's feelings, beliefs and will are the result of his place and circumstances of birth, the education given, and other circumstances not under his control. He is made what he is by other persons and does not make himself.[10] (2) Being the man that he is, it is inevitable that he fall into crime.[11] (3) To punish him for being what he did not choose to be, and could not have avoided, would be quite unjust.[12] To clinch the argument, Owen adds (4) The very people who punish him are the people (rulers, legislators, parents) who have—in part—made him what he is (by allowing him to be brought under crime-inducing conditions, by instilling in him false beliefs). They have made rules prohibiting him from doing that which, being the man he has been made by them, he will inevitably do.[13]

If in Owen's new society, there is to be no punishment, how are laws to be enforced and offenders handled? Owen wants to do away with laws in the ordinary acceptance of that term. The only kind of laws Owen wants do not require any enforcement. They are "nature's wise laws" which contrast with man's "irrational and absurd laws." The latter force men's naturally good "faculties, propensities and qualities" into an "unnatural channel." The former releases them. The object is to train them so that they are completely rational. When everybody is rational, only six laws will be necessary; these are "natural" laws; *i.e.*, laws which are in accordance with, not opposed to, human nature. One of these is that if by an outside chance "differences of opinion or feeling" should arise between (rational) men, they shall be arbitrated. This will "render all magistrates, lawyers, and

courts of law wholly unnecessary."[14] Punishment used in training
tends to make men, those who punish and those who are punished, unfit for such a rational world.

Is it possible for a man who has been given the proper surroundings and the right kind of training to commit an offense?
If so, what is to be done? Owen does not give us a clear answer
to our first question. In some places he says that all that is necessary is to give the proper training and that since man is naturally
good, he will not commit a crime. Owen would admit that a person who has been properly raised could commit an offense, but
only if he is mentally defective. To punish or blame a man would
be wrong. Yet, on the other hand, Owen must admit the possibility
that even in a colony of men properly raised and trained, there
might be deeds of which the government must take some kind
of cognizance. Owen's Sixth Law for the Governance of Men "in
accordance with the laws of their nature" reads:

> As any parties thus trained, educated, employed and placed
> who should act in opposition to the happiness of society indi-
> vidually or generally, could do so only by being afflicted with
> mental disease, individuals so acting shall be placed within a
> house of recovery, treated as mildly as the case will permit,
> and kept no longer within the house and its immediate and
> external enclosures than is necessary to reproduce a sound state
> of health.[15]

In the "General Rules and Regulations Proposed by Mr.
Owen For an Independent Community," we find, besides, the
following provision:[16] members may "explain" to a recalcitrant
"in what respect his conduct has been injurious, and at the same
time to intimate to him that unless the cause of complaint be
removed, they are instucted to expel him from the community."
But this rule Owen may have considered a transitory one, for a
community in which all the members have not had the benefit
of proper character training. We cannot help wondering how the
"House of Recovery" would have come to be regarded in Owen's
community if whenever a man "acts in opposition to the happiness of society" he is sent there; and we cannot but note that the
option of expelling a man from the community is not ordinarily
open to the government of the State as a way of coping with
undesirable behavior.

What is clearly valid in Owen's argument is this: if through no fault of their own, men possess certain characteristics, and if because of those characteristics they could not help breaking a given law, then it would be unjust to pass that law with penalty attached. This is a special case of the unjust way of legislating which we noticed in the fifth chapter: a special case of penalizing people for doing that which, if done, is not a moral offense.

It is possible to find clear cases of this: of men being what they are on account of circumstances outside their control, of their being thus unable to help breaking a given law, and thus of the law's being unjustly enacted. For example, laws might be passed making it a penal offense to be a Jew, or making it a penal offense to be unable to speak English. (These are rather crude examples. There would be no single law making it a penal offense to be a Jew, of course, but there would be a concatenation of laws—laws closing the schools and all sorts of employment and the right to purchase in certain stores to Jews—the net effect of which would be that it is against the law to be a Jew. Similarly, by legislation, life could be made impossible, in effect, for a person who did not know how to speak English. The injustice of the latter law presupposes of course that the person is not given time to learn to speak the language and that he is penalized immediately for his linguistic backwardness.) But Owen claims that criminals are, through no imputable fault, so constituted that they must break "man-made" laws; and that thus all criminal law and all punishment is unjust.

Let us try to understand what leads Owen to adopt such a position. When Owen talks about the people who commit crimes, he has in mind the lower classes. He has in mind particularly the underprivileged millworkers of his day, and more specifically yet the motley crew he found at his own mill at New Lanark, when he became manager there. Crime was an ordinary part of life for these people and the causes of it were evident to Owen: ignorance, long hours, drink, no recreation. He set out to remove these causes of crime, was very successful, and crime practically disappeared from New Lanark. Owen, by changing the conditions of life of these people, was able to eliminate crime. He did this by taking steps which any of the people in authority could have initiated. The conditions which Owen changed lay in plain view under the gaze of mill owners, magistrates, clergy and gentry.

Yet these people, the people in authority, did nothing to change them. But crime inevitably comes out of such circumstances, so the people in authority are responsible for the crime, not the lower classes who are allowed to come into the world and exist in circumstances which make crime inevitable. For these industrialists, land-owners, magistrates, and clergymen to insist on hanging for the stealing of goods from the bleaching grounds is for them to be if not morally wicked, at least morally obtuse.

II

Owen's intellectual descendants are those contemporary psychiatrists and criminologists[17] who contend that crime is not something imputable to the criminal, but, rather, to the criminal's abnormal condition: a condition brought on not by him, but by the circumstances of his life. To punish him is, therefore, unjust; what is neeeded is treatment.

Gregory Zilboorg tells us that the insistence upon punishment is a symptom of a pathological condition on the part of those who insist upon it.

> Our anxiety can be quieted down only in one of two ways: In our sudden unconscious denial of any similarity with the criminal we can hurl ourselves upon him with all the power of our aggressive, punitive, destructive hostility; or we can assume the criminal to be a mentally sick man and can then assume a more tolerant or charitable attitude toward the doer if not the deed.[18]

Walter Bromberg insists, in *Crime and The Mind*,[19] that: "A criminal act results when an impulse contrary to the expressed restrictions of civilized life cannot be withstood."[20] On this theory every crime results from the inability to abide by the law.

According to Benjamin Karpman,[21] "Criminal behavior is an unconsciously conditional psychic reaction over which (the criminals) have no conscious control." Karpman also tells us, "We have to treat them as psychically sick people which in every respect they are. It is no more reasonable to punish these individuals . . . than it is to punish an individual for breathing through his mouth because of enlarged adenoids, when a simple operation will do the trick."[22] We are told in a standard work on criminology,[23] "It seems not too much to expect society gradually to accept the thesis that the criminal also is socially ill and needs diagnosis and some sort of treatment other than punishment." The authors go on to argue that, "Most real criminals are so warped by their inherited defects or undesirable life habits, that their crimes are as natural an expression for them as law abiding conduct is for the rest of us."[24] If all criminals are sick, then obviously radical practical proposals about punishment follow. The most explicit of these proposals with which I am familiar was put forward as a resolution before the American Bar Association in 1926 by Carl Menninger.[25] In this proposal Menninger starts out by declaring that crime is only one type of "adaptation failure" with which the science of psychiatry is concerned, and that crime is, or can be, as an object of science, "studied, interpreted and controlled;" that science can change bad behavior, foresee it, and enable society to provide for it, and "detect and endeavor to prevent the development of potential criminality." Therefore, legal procedure and legislation must provide for psychiatry in court: "Ultimately a routine compulsory psychiatric examination of all offenders with latitude and *authority* in the recommendations made to the court as to the disposition and treatment of the prisoner." Menninger goes on.

> This also entails certain radical changes in penal practice including (a) substitution of the idea of treatment, painful or otherwise, for the idea of retributive punishment, (b) the release of prisoners upon discharge or parole only after complete and competent psychiatric examination with findings favorable for successful rehabilitation, to which end the desirability of resident psychiatrists in all penal institutions is obvious, (c) the permanent legal detention of the incurably inadequate, incompetent and anti-social, irrespective of the particular offense committed, (d) the use of this "permanently custodial group" for the advantage of the State—to earn their keep.

The alarm of many lawyers at such a proposal is understandable, especially when part (c) of the above recommendations is given serious consideration. The question arises how the rights of the criminal are protected if, at the will of a psychiatrist or Board of psychiatrists, he can be held in prison after the expiration of his term because that individual or Board finds that he is not "rehabilitated." If a man is to be permanently detained because he is "anti-social," it would seem that we would need a very clear definition of the word "anti-social": but no such definition has to this date been forthcoming.

Lawyers have hastened to remind their psychiatric opponents that there are more purposes in the criminal law than the rehabilitation of those who violate it.

> The social aspects to punishment have, for the most part, been ignored by their critics; their medical orientation serves to preoccupy them with the criminal *qua* patient. They forget that he is first a social unit and that although he may utimately be handed over to the doctor, demands of society ought first to be met. He does not have cancer or flu or dyspepsia; he has committed a crime, has injured someone, has damaged society according to its own definition. Because of this and irrespective of any moral taint, the criminal is obligated and must answer to society.[26]

By far the best reply to the psychiatrists with which I am acquainted is to be found in Hall's *Principles of Criminal Law*.[27] Hall challenges the right of the psychiatrist opponents of punishment to speak for science, or even for psychiatry; he underlines the lack of clear definition in psychiatric terminology and the resultant impossibility of substituting it for legal terms; he emphasizes the questionability of Freudian theories of human nature; and insists that a more adequate theory is embodied in the law.

The relevant discussion centers mainly on the psychiatrist-proposed Rule of "Irresistible Impulse" as a substitute for the generally accepted "M'Naghton Rules."[28] Most of the psychiatrists who would not go so far as White and Zilboorg in their insistence that crime is best understood as arising out of mental abnormality, are nevertheless in favor of substituting the Irresistible Impulse Rule for the M'Naghton Rules. Since the net result of the substitution would almost surely be a radical extension of the area of human action for which the agent cannot be held legally responsible, a brief survey of this dispute may be of interest before we turn to the underlying philosophical issues.[29]

The M'Naghton Rules were occasioned by the case of *The Queen v. M'Naghton*, 1843. M'Naghton having been acquitted of a sensational murder on the ground of insanity, a series of questions concerning the defense of insanity were put to the Lord Justices. After debate, they produced the answers which are still the most important part of the law on insanity in relation to criminal responsibility. The central assertion of these rules is that

> To establish a defense on the ground of insanity, it must be clearly proved that, at the time of the committing of the act, the party accused was labouring under such a defect of reason, from disease of the mind, as not to know the nature and quality of the act he was doing; or, if he did know it, that he did not know he was doing what was wrong.

The objection to this rule, on the part of psychiatrists and other interested parties has been mainly that many criminals are compulsives: that is, many if not most of those who are really insane *know* that what they are doing is wrong, but *cannot* refrain from doing the act anyway. Further there are many insane persons who do criminal acts *because* they know that they are wrong, and because they want to expiate a sense of guilt by drawing the resultant punishment upon themselves. Such persons, it is argued, should not be punished but should instead be treated for mental disorder.[30] The test, says an early writer in the field,[31] should not be ". . . whether the individual be conscious of right or wrong—not whether he had a knowledge of the consequences of his act—but whether he can properly control his action." The difficulty with such a criterion is that it is not clear how we are to distinguish inability to resist an impulse from simple failure to resist it. Was the impulse irresistible or simply not resisted? Clear answers to this difficulty have not been forthcoming. If the question of insanity turns on the commission of the very deed which the criminal has done, how are we to prevent the distinction from exonerating as insane whatever is done on "impulse?" It will not do either to say that the commission of like acts in the past indicates "irresistible impulse," for this may just as well indicate habit and it seems odd to try to get a man off of a murder charge on the sole ground that he has committed a number of murders in the past.

Because the rule of "irresistible impulse" is on his view untenable, Hall finds himself inclined to accept the M'Naghton

Rules as interpreted by enlightened judges, as the best criterion of insanity offered to date. Desirable reforms in this rule are, he feels, delayed because the proposed reforms have so far been coupled with a theory (of "irresistible impulse") which attacks the very foundations of criminal responsibility.

III

Two issues must be distinguished in the "treatment vs. punishment" argument. One is the prudential issue: whether crime would be more diminished by treatment than by punishment. The other is the moral issue: whether if (as contended) the criminal is not responsible for his crime, there is any justice in punishing him. Important as the first question is, I cannot deal with it here. Sweeping claims have been made for the superior efficacy of treatment in the reduction of crime. The evaluation of these claims would require careful analysis of experimental data. It may be doubted whether there is enough data upon which to found any very firm conclusion. The enterprise will be hampered, also, by the theoretical difficulties, to be noted below, in distinguishing between treatment and punishment.

What leads many people to favor treatment over punishment is not a prudential but a moral belief: that punishment is no longer justified since whereas we had assumed criminals responsible for their crimes, we have now discovered that the assumption is at best shaky, and at worst false. In examining the contention that criminals (or most of them) are not (or not to the extent that we had thought) responsible for their crimes, we will try to keep the discussion on a plane sufficiently general to include the contentions of those, earlier, "positivists" whom we have not specifically recognized in our remarks above.[32]

The first point that should be noted is how far the purported discovery about the responsibility of criminals spreads. Criminals are distinguished from other human beings by their having committed a crime; and it is at least in principle possible to enact laws in such fashion that, descriptively speaking, any deed whatever is prohibited, and thus made criminal. So to say that no criminals are responsible for their crimes (or most are not) is to say, whether the implication is drawn out or not, that no one (or few people) are responsible for their actions. And this implication may be accepted or even welcomed. It may be well to pause over it.

The remark that no one is (or few people are) responsible for their actions is sometimes offered as if it were in the same logical category with remarks like "No one has brown eyes," or "No one in Texas is under six feet tall." But whereas we can easily picture a world in which there are no people with brown eyes, and even more easily picture a Texas in which there are no people under six feet, we do not find it so easy to picture a world in which no one is responsible. And this difficulty comes not from our lack of "picturing ability" but from a logical uncertainty. This logical uncertainty arises because the way in which the word "responsible" is being used has not been made clear.

It is not the specification of a world to say that in it no one will be responsible. This is simply a way of talking, and what must be determined is what kind of situation it is in which this way of talking has a place, and what kind of place it is. A natural response to the contention that no one is responsible is to throw up one's hands in horror at the notion of such a world. But this is a mistaken response, for the world at which one is throwing up one's hands is not yet specified, by saying that in it no one is responsible.

Some people have brown eyes, and we can sensibly imagine a world in which there are no people with brown eyes. Some people are responsible for their deeds. Why can we not sensibly imagine a world in which no people are responsible for their deeds? It is not what we can imagine but what we can understand that is the issue. We can understand the contention that for some scientific reason or other it is likely that within twenty-five years everybody still living will have blue eyes, but what kind of scientific reason would be given for showing that within twenty-five years no one will be responsible for anything?

While we may not be clear on the use which is being given to "responsible" in "No one is responsible for crime;" there is one point about this use on which we *are* clear: it does not correspond to any of the ordinary uses of the word. In the ordinary uses there is a tacit reference to such recognized heads of exception as mistake, accident, infancy, insanity, when it is claimed either that a person is not responsible for a given deed or is not responsible in general (dispositionally). But if the very same reason serves to exonerate every one from responsibility, then this reason is no longer a head of exception. Therefore, though in the ordinary acceptance of the term it follows from "A is not responsible" that "A ought not to be punished;" the implication cannot be assumed to hold where "responsible" is given a totally different use. We cannot even assume that the first statement is a reason for the second. We simply do not know if the first statement is a reason for the second, because we do not know the rules which govern the "discussion game" which is apparently here being initiated: in fact we do not know whether there *are* any rules, and therefore whether there is a "game" at all. We can only speculate about the circumstances in which the indicated "game" might arise, and how it might be conducted.

If we are to understand the contention that psychiatry and sociology have discovered that criminals are not responsible, or that few of them are responsible, we must know more about what it means to say of a person that he is or is not responsible. Ascriptions of responsibility are, in fact, like justifications of punishment, a varied and extensive lot. We have no more right to assume that there is one abstract general responsibility-ascription than we have to assume that there is one such punishment-justification.[33]

In the first place, we speak of persons as being, in general, responsible (that is, as being the sort of person to whom responsibilities can be entrusted without worry). Secondly, we speak of a person's being responsible *for* something—in a variety of ways. He can be responsible *for* the performance of certain tasks (watering the horses), all of the tasks in a given area of common endeavor (for the livestock), or—in a connected way—for the performance of his subordinates (for the cowhands). These are prospective or a-temporal ascriptions of responsibility. But there are also retrospective ascriptions.

We can say that A is responsible *for* something that *has happened* (B's death). To say this is to pack together some or all of a number of articles in a single suitcase. It may be to say that: (1) A *caused* the event to occur (was, in legal jargon, the "real," "leading," or "proximate" cause—not merely a causal condition, like the operation of the laws of gravity). (2) That A is *at fault* for what occurred (he placed the hammer near the edge of the platform and it fell off; he flung it in the air as a joke; he aimed and threw it). (3) That A is *answerable* for what happened (he is subject to blame, and/or to execution, imprisonment, the payment of indemnity).

A can be held legally answerable for what (a) he did not cause, or (b) he is not at fault for causing. (a) He can be made answerable for the acts of his servants or employees, the misbehavior of his dogs, the mistakes of his accountant. (b) It may well be that A would not be held to be at fault for any of the above-mentioned acts which he did not cause, but in addition he may be held answerable for what he did indeed cause, but was not at fault for causing. Thus, *e.g.*, A sold the drug which, misused by C in violation of A's instructions, killed B; or A put up the road sign which caused B to take the highway on which, because a bridge collapsed, B is killed; or A ordered B to come down from an icy structure, and on the way B slipped and was killed.

A *may* be held legally answerable for what he did or did not cause, and for which he is or is not at fault. Therefore to determine whether A is answerable for B's death, it is enough to determine that he caused it and/or is at fault for it. It is the retributivist position that fault is both necessary and sufficient ground for answerability. There does not seem to be any single utilitarian position. If there is utilitarian value in strict liability, and if strict liability can be interpreted so strictly that there is no fault left,[34] then fault is not—on utilitarian grounds—a necessary condition of answerability. In any case, it is not sufficient.

The argument against the institution of legal punishment based on the premise that no one is (or very few people are) responsible for crime needs, then, a great deal more development than it has received. What is meant by saying that no one is (or few are) responsible for crime? It cannot be meant that people are not responsible in the causal sense of that word. Nor can it be meant that they are not answerable: it is surely not being denied that people are in fact *held* responsible (liable) for certain events. It must be in the sense of the imputation of fault. The contention is, then, that no one is (or few are) at fault for the violation of criminal laws. But if this is what is meant, is the discovery in question properly regarded as a scientific discovery? It is hard, in the first place, to know how far the discovery extends. As noted above, in principle any kind of deed could be prohibited or required by law. So, in principle, it would follow that no one is (or few are) at fault for the commission of any deed whatever. Secondly, it is generally conceded that the question whether or not a person is at fault is a moral rather than a scientific question (whatever may be the grounds on which such a distinction is made).

Even supposing we should grant that it has been "discovered" that no one is (or few are) responsible (meaning, *at fault*) for his crime, then it does not follow immediately that no one should be punished. For what must now be shown is that only those persons who are at fault should be punished.This is a premise which retributivists would accept; but utilitarians might not accept. It has been generally overlooked, I think, that the attack on the institution of legal punishment under discussion hereby assumes a basic premise of the retributivistic justification of that institution, even though it is the retributivist view of punishment (assumed incorrectly to provide its only support) which is at the same time attacked. But since no clear sense has been given to the "discovery" in question, it is not clear what we are conceding, even for the sake of argument.

We have tried to show, so far, that: (a) the scientific status of the "discovery" that all (or most) men are not responsible for their crimes is questionable;[35] and (b) the assumption that there shall be answerability only where the act is caused by the agent and/or is his fault, is also questionable.

Perhaps these difficulties are surmountable. Suppose that the "treatment" advocate recognizes and accepts his agreement with the retributivists that fault is a necessary (if not sufficient) condition of answerability. We have pointed out the debatability of this assumption, and the absence of its defense in the "treatment" position. But it *could* be recognized and defended.[36] Suppose he also retreats from his position that the narrowing of the area of responsibility is a "scientific discovery." What would remain? Much which is worthy of careful attention.

The advocate of "treatment" would then frankly admit that his position is primarily a moral one, and not something which he knows on scientific grounds to be correct. What he does still claim to know scientifically is that all or most crime is committed by persons in some way deficient. His moral contention is that this deficiency constitutes an excuse for the commission of the crime; the crime is not therefore the fault of the person committing it; and punishment would therefore be unjust.

There must then be offered affirmative grounds for the substitution of treatment for punishment in most or all cases. What would have to be shown is that the deficiencies in question are such as are likely to respond to treatment, and that the appropriate treatment is known and could be made available. Finally, it would have to be shown that, granting the treatment is available, the principle that all or most criminals should be treated can be defended against charges of injustice sure to arise.

In closing we will list some of the difficulties which this more candid and carefully stated "treatment" position would have to meet. (1) What are the deficiencies suffered by all or most criminals?[37] (2) Since, in principle, any description of deed can be prohibited or enjoined by law, and crime consists in violation of law; is it contended that the deficiency in question is shared by everyone? If so, in what sense is it a deficiency?[38] (3) Would a "deficiency" shared by everyone, or almost everyone, consitute an excuse? Mistake of fact, accident, coercion, duress, provocation, insanity; and infancy are excuses which are accepted in criminal law as excluding or reducing liability to punishment. If infancy, e.g., were extended to include all but senile persons (as senility is presently understood), would it then be an excuse? To say, Yes, is to abolish punishment. But, is the decision to abolish punishment to be made on this ground alone? And what would it mean to treat all or most people as if they were infants—or insane, not only in the courts but in everyday life? And if the distinction is not extended to everyday life, what happens to the contention that the deficiency in question excuses by showing that the person in question was not at fault? (4) Is treatment necessarily more just in execution than punishment? Suppose that Menninger's proposals[39] had been accepted. Would there be no ground for complaints of injustice on the part of criminals restrained against their wills for (sometimes unpleasant) treatment until the (sometimes difficult to define) deficiency in question is removed? Would it be possible in such cases to distinguish between treatment and punishment?

Until the "treatment" position has been more adequately presented, and the obvious difficulties met; and on the principle that the burden of proof should be on him who proposes a change; it would seem the part of wisdom not to move very fast toward the substitution of treatment for punishment.

CHAPTER VI

FOOTNOTES

1. *The Life of Robert Owen*, London, 1857, Vol. I, p. 11.
2. *Essays on the Formation of the Human Character*, p. 14.
3. *Ibid.*, pp. 208-209.
4. *Ibid.*, p. 209.
5. *Ibid.*, Introduction, 1st paragraph.
6. *Essays*, p. 36. Cf. also, *The Book of the New Moral World*, p. 5. "It is for acts of the will that men are punished or rewarded by men; because they have hitherto imagined that the will was formed by the voluntary impulse of the individual."
7. *The Book*, p. 26.
8. *Ibid.*, Section Headings, pp. 17-26, and *Essays*, p. 6.
9. *Ibid.*, p. 190, Section 10; *Essays*, p. 5. "ANY GENERAL CHARACTER FROM THE BEST TO THE WORST, FROM THE MOST IGNORANT TO THE MOST ENLIGHTENED MAY BE GIVEN TO ANY COMMUNITY EVEN TO THE WORLD AT LARGE BY THE APPLICATION OF THE PROPER MEANS: WHICH MEANS ARE TO A GREAT EXTENT AT THE COMMAND AND UNDER THE CONTROL OF THOSE WHO HAVE INFLUENCE IN THE AFFAIRS OF MEN."
10. *Ibid.*, pp. 15-26; *Essays*, p. 47.
11. *Ibid.*, p. 31. "Man cannot therefore be bad by nature; and it must be a gross error to make him responsible for what nature and his predecessors have compelled him to. . . . It is . . . cruel and unjust in the extreme still further to afflict and punish a poor individual, after he has been already ill treated by nature and the society in which his character has been formed from birth." Cf. also, *Essays*, p. 14.
12. Cf. quotations and references in the two footnotes just above.
13. *Essays*, p. 6. "Nor will it be possible hereafter for comparatively a few individuals unintentionally to occasion the rest of mankind to be surrounded by circumstances which inevitably form such characters as they afterwards deem it a duty and a right to punish even to death; and that too, while they themselves have been the instruments of forming those characters." Cf. also, *Essays*, p. 28, and quote from *The Book* in note No. 7 above.
14. *The Book of the New Moral World*, VI, IV *passim*; p. 114.
15. *Ibid.*, p. 114.
16. Rule XXXIII.
17. As will be apparent below, I do not wish to imply that all psychiatrists and criminologists, or even the majority, would defend the position described below. Nor do I wish to restrict the position to psychiatrists and criminologists. A few lawyers and jurists have taken up something very much like it. But the position described is philosophically interesting, for it represents one possible extreme on the question of criminal responsibility and answerability; and the problems which it raises will be central for less extreme, more guarded, positions.
18. *The Psychology of The Criminal Act and Punishment*, New York, 1954, p. 80.

19. Philadelphia, 1948.
20. p. 177.
21. "Criminality, Insanity and The Law," *Journal of Criminal Law and Criminology*, 1939, p. 584.
22. *Ibid.*
23. H. E. Barnes and N. K. Teeters, *New Horizons in Criminology*, New York, 1943, p. 952.
24. *Ibid.*, pp. 952-53.
25. Carl A. Menninger, "The Psychiatrist in Relation to Crime," *American Bar Association Reports*, LI (1926), pp. 751-57.
26. Edward De Grazia, "Crime Without Punishment: A Psychiatric Conundrum," 52 *Columbia Law Review* 754 (1952).
27. Jerome Hall, *General Principles of Criminal Law*, 2nd edition, Indianapolis, New York, 1960. Chapter 13.
28. I shall ignore the so-called Durham "Product" Rule, which, of recent origin and narrow acceptance, seems to raise no new philosophical (even though grave practical) issues.
29. Cf., Hall, *op. cit.*
30. Perhaps the historically most influential presentation of this argument is in a book published in 1896, and widely quoted: H. Maudsley, *Responsibility in Mental Disease* (New York, D. Appleton & Company). In this book Maudsley (a professor of medical jurisprudence at University College, London) offers a variety of case histories especially of murderers and suicides to show that a man may, while knowing and acknowledging the wrongness of his deeds, nevertheless be unable to restrain the impulse which "forces" him to do it. In these cases the criminal will typically be quite sane in every respect except that he feels a powerful urge to commit a certain sort of crime. Maudsley considers the person who possesses such an urge (too powerful to be kept always under control) as mentally diseased. He strengthens his argument by showing that very often such urges are "substitutions" in later life for epileptic seizure (admittedly a disease) in early life. He also argues that persons afflicted by such urges often are descended from mentally diseased parents. (Cf. especially Chapters 4, 5, 7 and 9).
31. Knaggs, *Responsibility in Criminal Lunacy*, 1854, p. 69 (quoted in Hall op. cit., p. 487).
32. "Positivist" is the name usually given a group of sociologists and jurists mostly Italian late 19th—early 20th century. They are united in the belief that criminals as a group have common scientifically determinable characteristics, other than their violation of the law. They believe that the punishment should be made to "fit the criminal" rather than the crime: on the theory that the main object of criminal law is to reform criminals. They differed radically in their conceptions of the common characteristics of the "criminal class" as well as in their ideas concerning treatment of that class. Cesare Lombroso (Cf. Gina Lombroso Ferrero, *Criminal Man According to the Classification of Cesare Lombroso*, Putnam, New York, 1911) believed criminals were a definite biological type having cauliflower ears, low foreheads and too many digits on the hands. Garofalo (Raffaele Garofalo, *Criminology*, Robert W. Millar (trans.), Boston, 1914) classified criminals on psychological rather than physiological grounds. He held that what distinguishes them as a class is a deficiency in "pity or probity." Ferri (Enrico Ferri, *Criminal Sociology*, J. F. Kelly and J. Lisle, translators, Boston, 1917) emphasized besides the biological and psychological characteristics of the criminal, the sociological background of crime. He was a pioneer in his insistence that the way to attack crime is by such methods as encouraging birth control and allowing unrestricted emigration. None of these men, except perhaps Lombroso in his earlier days, would have claimed that the persons who commit crimes are invariably born, psychologically inclined, or sociologically conditioned to do so; and that therefore they should not be held responsible. But they do make of the "normal" criminal a minor class; and they do hold

that the class of persons not responsible for their crimes is enormously larger than we had thought.

33. In the analysis of responsibility which follows, I am heavily indebted to Professor Joel Feinberg of Princeton University. But he is not "responsible" for the distinctions made here.

34. Richard A. Wasserstrom, "Strict Liability in the Criminal Law," *Stanford Law Review,* XII, 1960, pp. 730-45. Reprinted in Herbert Morris, ed. *Freedom and Responsibility,* Stanford University Press, Stanford, California, 1961, pp. 273-281.

35. For another line of argument leading to the same conclusion, Cf. my article, "Responsibility, Insanity, and Psychological Discovery," *Darshana,* August, 1962, pp. 84-88.

36. As, *e.g.,* in Chapter VII.

37. It should be noted that the nominations for these deficiencies have changed with the times.

38. Compare, "the trauma of birth."

39. *Supra,* p. 103.

CHAPTER VII

THE JUSTIFICATION OF PUNISHMENT

By what right do some people punish others?

TOLSTOY

No one can know how many reasons there are or might be for wishing to modify or reject punishment. And as we offer the case for the institution of legal punishment, we wish to reveal as candidly as possible the vulnerable underpinnings on which the argument rests. For it is not a justification for all space and time, but one which applies only under certain conditions. These conditions are not local or peculiar, but it is easy to conceive of a world in which they did not obtain.

I

What, in principle, would constitute an adequate defense of the institution of legal punishment? Before attempting an answer we must raise a prior question: What kind of undertaking *is* a "defense" or "justification" of an institution or practice?[1] Not, how do we go about it? But, what is it we are going about?

We are offering reasons for the conclusion that punishment should be retained not abolished. In doing so, we are thinking of the practice of punishment not as a rib of the universe, but as a device which serves certain purposes well or ill. It is not a device in the sense that it is a "dodge" or "gadget" which can be used today and abandoned tomorrow. But it is something which has been devised—not all at once, or consciously, perhaps; but it is an invention of man. It is an arrangement which we (the writer and most of the readers of this book) find already present in the culture of which we become bearers; but our culture could have been otherwise. There are cultures in which there is no legal punishment. To justify legal punishment is, then, to show that there are better reasons for retaining than for abolishing it.

Strictly speaking, if we subscribe to the principle that the burden of proof is on him who would institute a change; all that is necessary in the defense of a going practice is to show that no adequate grounds for changing it have been brought forward. But it is not merely because it is there, and change always makes difficulties, that punishment should be retained. A positive case can be made out for it which would warrant instituting legal punishment if it were not already the practice.

How, then, should we go about offering a justification of legal punishment? What, in principle, would constitute an adequate general defense or justification of punishment or of any social practice?[2] To justify a practice is to show two things: that under the circumstances, a practice is necessary, called for, or would be useful; and that of the alternatives available and acceptable, the practice in question would likely be the most effective. We will refer to the reason why some practice must be instituted as the "guiding principle" of justification; and to the considerations by reference to which the practice is rejected as nonacceptable even though it seems the best of the available alternatives, in the light of the guiding principle, as the "limiting principles" of justification. It is with respect to the guiding principle that a proposed practice can be more or less effective; but it may be rejected, even though effective, by a limiting principle.

These are general formal conditions of the justification of a practice. It is a necessary condition of an adequate justification of a practice that of the available alternatives it most efficiently serves the purpose for which a practice is needed; it is a necessary condition that the practice not be ruled out by a limiting principle; and it is a necessary and sufficient condition that the practice serve the purpose as well as possible within the bounds set by the limiting principles.[3] This schema is at least useful in approaching the problem of the justification of a specific practice. It forces us to distinguish between the questions whether a practice is necessary; whether the practice in question best fills the need; and if, even so, it must be rejected.

But Tolstoy's question, with which we wish to come to grips in this chapter, concerns the right to punish. It requests a specifically moral justification. Like an economic or aesthetic justification of a practice, a moral justification will have guiding and limiting principles. But whatever principles we accept must be shown to be *morally* defensible. This may seem to present insuperable difficulties, for there are apparently irreconcilable differences over the ultimate principles of morality. Hence, what is morally defensible to one school will not be so to another. Utilitarians, self-realizationalists, intuitionists might fail to agree on the moral defensibility of the guiding and limiting principles by which punishment must be morally assessed as a practice. It may come out this way. But it may not. What is morally defensible from one point of view need not be indefensible from another. And it may be that the schema we use will point up the complementarity rather than the incompatibility of the leading moral views. For who wishes to deny that a practice must be shown to serve some purpose? The retributivist can, as we have seen, argue with real plausibility, that particular decisions concerning punishments should not be made on the ground that some supposedly good purpose would be served by punishing. And the retributivist can argue (less plausibly I believe) that all penal laws should be passed solely on the ground that justice demands them.

But is it really plausible to argue that justice demands *a* practice? Is it not more plausible to argue that when a practice can be shown to be necessary on utilitarian grounds, it should meet the demands of justice? Does justice demand the institution or practice of law, or marriage, or private property, or coined money? Or, at least, that there should be *an* institution which serves the purposes served by these? To say Yes, is to say that there are burdens and privileges existing prior to an institution or practice, which the practice should be invented and adopted to protect. But then the question is how we can know what these burdens and privileges are, prior to any practice within which they operate. To say that the institution should be invented and adopted to protect these burdens and privileges is like saying that basketball should be invented so that fouls and points for goals can be recognized and penalized or rewarded. But, outside of basketball there are no fouls and points for goals. What would it mean to say that there are burdens and privileges which persons have, to protect which it is essential that we adopt the practice of marriage?

This might seem more plausible with respect to punishment.

Is punishment as an institution justified because justice demands that there should be an institution which accords punishment to ill desert? The ill desert must then be supposed to exist independently of any practice in terms of which it can be defined. The crucial point here is that it is impossible to account for the *existence* of desert in the absence of a practice in terms of which desert can be assigned. What may lead us to think that desert can exist independently of a given punishment-practice is that desert is a concept in not one but several practices: legal punishment being merely the most clearly articulated of them. But if we stop to think of it we would realize that we could not speak, for example, of what Johnny deserves for pouring ink on the oriental rug were it not for *some* prior understanding of a practice. According to this practice, those persons playing the role of parent are given the authority to assign penalties not only for certain kinds of acts in advance, but also for acts adjudged "bad" or "naughty" after the fact: like pouring ink on rugs or putting glue in the seats. Punishment of such acts is justified, even though there is no rule promulgated in advance against them. But whence do parents derive the moral authority to identify and punish such acts? Surely not from some table beyond the tables of rules. Then we would simply have to ask for the credentials of that table, and of any table from which it was derived, and so on. It is not that the ill desert exists prior to the role of parent, but that parents are persons who are given discretion, according to a practice, to make decisions concerning ill desert.

It might seem that, nevertheless, there is ill desert independent of the practices of punishment, because the decisions of parents or judges are not merely arbitrary: decisions concerning desert are not right simply by virtue of being made by the proper authorities, but by virtue of being made in accordance with standards which the authorities should observe. We can criticize the authority's decisions on rational grounds. But the analogous point holds for fouls in basketball, or balls and strikes in baseball. Here too we can criticize the decision of the umpire by reference to the criteria by which he should be governed. But it does not follow that there could be balls and strikes were there no game of baseball. The assertion that a person deserves severe punishment is significant if and only if there is some practice according to which some authority could, by discoverable criteria, rightly award severe punishment. To say that justice is a limiting principle of possible practices of punishment is not to say that practices should somehow meet the requirement that some abstract, extra-practice "desert" should be given its due. It is but to say that the practice must, in virtue of its arrangements, give everyone concerned a fair shake. This point will be expanded below.

II

Let us now turn to the question what the circumstances are which give rise to the need for some practice, be it legal punishment, or an alternative. Here we will list certain very general assumptions of fact which, taken together, give rise to the problem. To the extent that these assumptions of fact are shaky, the justification of punishment totters; for the problem punishment and its competing practices are designed to meet alters or disappears. The assumptions of fact in question fall naturally into three different categories: assumptions concerning human nature, human society, and nature or "supernature."

Concerning human nature, we assume that humans are non-ant-like in that they do not order their affairs by instinct: *i.e.*, without rules. We assume also that whatever rules or regulations men set for themselves, there will be tension between the rules and the private interests, desires, or passions of persons falling under these rules: that there will not be automatic submission.

Concerning human society we assume that it is necessary to set some rules if men wish to survive, simply because human beings, being without enough instinctual equipment, are incapable of carrying on common activities necessary for their survival unless they are shown, told, taught, how to conduct themselves, what to do, and what to refrain from doing. And we assume that it is *desirable* to set *other* rules if the common life is to enhance the well-being (however that is defined) and reduce the misery and unhappiness (easier to agree upon) of all.

Concerning nature or "supernature," we assume that no natural or supernatural forces either compel action in accordance with the rules, or counter each violation with retribution. Lightning does not, as a matter of course, strike down either the man whose hand is raised with murderous intention or the murderer whose intention has been fulfilled. If lightning, pestilence, or tornado operated in either of these ways, social arrangements to ensure compliance with rules would be redundant.

To these factual assumptions we must now add a moral one. We assume that survival in conditions not merely miserable, and with some hope of happiness, is a value worthy of protection. We shall assume, indeed, that to interfere with these modest prospects and possibilities is morally wrong; and that each community has a collective moral right to prevent such interference.

Granting, then, that men wish to survive, and to decrease their misery and enhance their well-being there must be rules; and some social arrangement must be found which will counter the tendency to violate rules. Two points should be noted here. The arrangement in question is not required to be one which equally discourages the violation of all rules; some rules are more important for survival and well-being than others; and the effectiveness needed in the prevention of some rule-violations is not demanded for the prevention of all rule-violations. And, whatever practice may be instituted, its application in the prevention of rule-violations will be justified only to the extent that the rule and/or rule-set is justified. This latter point must be expanded.

Legislators[4] may be in a position to enact any rules they choose. In enacting rules, they may or may not have sufficiently in mind the survival or well-being of the citizens. Their laws may be designed to enhance their own well-being. The state may be administered like the legislators' private plantation, the citizens regarded as serfs—and it may be badly administered even on these terms. Can any practice designed to encourage compliance with the rules of such a legislature be justified? The alternative practices in question are not designed to encourage compliance with any particular set of rules, but are devices to encourage compliance with *rules*. To show that there may be bad rules is not to show that the practices are bad practices. The practices are *needed* to counter the tendency to violate rules which for our survival and well-being we must have; but this, unfortunately, does not prevent their *being used* to enforce rules which may even go against the ends of survival and well-being. To reject them on this account is like rejecting hammers because they may be used by murderers, or representative government because we disapprove of the Senator from Mississippi.

There is a limit beyond which this argument should not be

pressed. For telling counter-examples can be given. Should we not reject the practice of carrying hand-guns, *e.g.*, even though it arose for a defensible set of purposes: to provide a light gun, capable of being carried on long trips, which can be used for small game and, in wild country, for self-defense? Should we not have rejected duelling, even though it may originally have been a desirable substitute for simple unorganized mayhem? But the analogous argument in the present discussion would have to show that the conditions which gave rise to the demand for a practice designed to encourage compliance with rules are now so changed that practices originally meeting that need are now needed and are used for unjustifiable ends. While this does not now seem a plausible pair of contentions, it should be conceded that they could be, under circumstances now hard to foresee. If the great majority of human beings were in some way transformed so that the tension between rules and personal interests, passions, and desires disappeared; then the circumstances which gave rise to the need for a practice would have disappeared. And it could be that, under those circumstances, the practices originally designed to encourage compliance with rules, and now no longer necessary, were being used instead merely as instruments of oppression.

III

Suppose it be granted that, conditions being what they are, some practice to encourage compliance with rules is needed. Should punishment be preferred to other possible practices? Before attempting to assess the relative merits and demerits of punishment and its competitors, we must discuss the grounds of comparison. These, as we have noted, concern effectiveness and acceptability.

Punishment is *not* the most effective possible method for discouraging crime. Probably the most effective way to discourage —better, abolish—crime is to annihilate the human race. Or if this seems a little extreme, no doubt we could go a long way toward the elimination of crime by the use of drugs: the tranquilization of the human race. These possibilities are mentioned to point up the absurdity of arguing solely on grounds of effectiveness in the reduction of crime. Even though the procedures mentioned would work to eliminate crime, they would not be acceptable. What are the boundaries of acceptability? To what limiting principles may we appeal in rejecting an effective practice?[5]

Above, we mentioned not only justice but also humanity. By denominating humanity a limiting principle, we mean that one possible ground for refusal to accept an effective practice is that it is inhumane. It is apparently usually assumed in theoretical writing that any practice which is inhumane is by the same token unjust, since humanity as a separate limiting principle is not discussed. Yet it is not absurd to suppose that a given practice could be just but inhumane: that it might violate none of the maxims of justice and still demand treatment of individuals which we would agree is cruel or degrading. The "solution" of the problem of crime by annihilation or drugging could be not only effective, but just—in that it did not violate any of the maxims of justice by discriminating between persons: drugging or annihilating everyone impartially. This possibility gives rise to the maxim that justice should be "tempered with mercy"—and to a certain confusion attending this maxim. For justice is not inherently opposed to mercy: what is just may be humane enough; but it need not be humane at all.

How is it to be decided whether a proposed practice is inhumane? It will not do to speak briskly of setting up cardinal or ordinal scales on which there is a zero mark between minus-inhumane degrees and positive-humane ones. The question would then be how we know where to place any practice on the scale. Is it possible to find a purely formal criterion of inhumanity in a practice? It may be, but if so it would have to be developed in conjunction with a criterion of the justice of a practice, to which problem we now turn.

What is it for a practice to be just?[6] We shall take it that a practice is just if, knowing that it is necessary that there should be *a* practice and that this one would be effective, each of us would be willing to accept the practice not knowing in advance what role we would play. To expand: the assessment of the justice of a practice involves the conception of a particular view of the practice. It is the view taken of it by a person who realizes that a practice is necessary, and that this one will fulfill the need; who also realizes that in any practice there are going to be burdens and privileges;[7] and who must decide whether these privileges and burdens are fairly apportioned in view of what the practice is designed to accomplish. The test of fairness of apportionment of burdens and privileges is whether the person contemplating the practice would be willing to commit himself to it not knowing which role he might have to play; not from benevolence or self-sacrifice, but because he, along with everyone else, needs the practice.

Our hypothetical uncommitted person might be unwilling to commit himself to a proposed practice for fear of discrimination, not only within, but in assignment to the roles of the practice; and these two types of discrimination are worth distinguishing here. I might be able to predict now that I would (because of the color of my skin, say) be more likely than other persons to be assigned a given burdened role in a proposed practice (criminal, defendant). Or the role itself (slave) might be such that whoever has to play it is the victim of discrimination, no matter how effective the practice may seem for no matter what good purposes. Slavery, then, may doubly discriminate: in its choice of persons to play the burdened role, and in its allocation of burdens and privileges between roles. It is with discrimination in the second sense that the justice of practices is, strictly speaking, concerned. But by thinking whether a person situated as described could agree to the practice; we will not lose sight of the first form of discrimination either.

We may now return to the question of the criterion of humanity. More accurately, what is wanted is a criterion or criteria by reference to which it can be determined whether a practice is inhumane. Duelling may be a useful example. It is one of the several alternative practices by which quarrels can be settled.[8] A practice was needed. Whether it was a just practice may be questioned. That it was inhumane to cause a man to lose his life as the price of losing an argument, seems clear—to us, here, now. Why, on what ground, would we call it inhumane? It was not inhumane in that it resulted in the loss of life. Lives were lost in the transportation of freight from harbor to harbor; and the practice of exchanging goods was not on that account inhumane. Duelling was inhumane because it resulted in *unnecessary* mutilation, suffering, degradation, and loss of life: unnecessary because there were available equally efficient and just ways of settling quarrels.

There is another way in which a practice can impose unnecessary, and thus inhumane, degradation, suffering, or death:
it can be, unlike duelling, a practice which serves no necessary
purpose at all. It is hard to think of examples, partly because
when a practice becomes a part of the way of life of a people it
begins to play roles not originally envisaged for it, even if it ceases
to be needed for the original purposes. But unless we are willing
to subscribe to the thesis, so far as practices are concerned, that
whatever is is right, there will be ritual and other practices which
because of the degradation and suffering they cause individuals
falling under them are inhumane and hence no longer acceptable.
Examples might be the *suttee*, and the taking of heads as trophies.

If the criterion of inhumanity in a practice is to be that suffering, misery, death or degradation are imposed unnecessarily;
then what is a test by which we can know that a given practice
is inhumane? Analogously to the test for injustice of a practice,
we can ask whether a person, acknowledging the need for practice, acknowledging that this practice would be efficient in ful-
filling that need, acknowledging that the practice in question
fairly distributes the burdens and privileges it creates, would
nevertheless not want to commit himself to the practce on the
ground that there are other equally efficient and fair practices
which do not (as this one does) impose suffering, misery, degradation or death.[9]

IV

We may now return to the justification of legal punishment.
We have tried to show that *a* practice is needed, and we have
tried to specify criteria of comparison between punishment and
alternative practices. What alternative practices are available,
and how do they compare to punishment in the light of these
criteria?

We will not here attempt to cover all the kinds of practice
which would be used to encourage compliance with rules, but
will limit ourselves to those which presuppose a system of law.
We are thus taking it for granted that it is not only advantageous
to have rules but to have legal rules. Our only excuse for such
a leap is that to do more than sketch, as we have done, the general justification of rules, is to embark on a question, the justifi-

cation of law, which cannot be handled within the scope of this book. A full answer to Owen and Tolstoy, who attack the system of law as well as punishment, would require a very much larger book than this one.

There is in principle no limit to the devices which human imagination could create for encouraging compliance with legal rules. Some of these we have noted (and rejected) in passing, such as telishment, the practices which would make of judges or legislators mere social engineers or mere balancers of the scales of justice, and "treatment." There are at least four remaining general sorts of practice which should be mentioned: 1) Practices which punish failure to comply with the law by informal means rather than the formal procedure of legal punishment involving legislators, judges, and jailers. Varieties of social suasion other than punishment have been described for us by cultural anthropologists; and while (is this analytic?) there will be no statutes in preliterate tribes, it is conceivable that social suasion could be relied upon to enforce statutes. For example, it might be the practice that if a man commits incest, he is shamed in public by anyone knowing of the deed; or if he fails to support his in-laws his wife will leave him. 2) Practices according to which compliance with the law is rewarded. 3) Practices according to which men are persuaded to abide by the law. 4) Practices according to which men are conditioned (drugs, neo-Pavlovian techniques) to obey the law. Of these, all are really consistent with legal punishment. And "adequate" is to be understood in terms of the criteria already mentioned.

Social suasion is perhaps the strongest candidate of the four. What is envisaged is the possibility that criminal statutes should be enacted with no penalty attached; that courts should decide guilt but not sentence; that, instead, suitable publicity should be given the crime, and the criminal returned to home and community. The assumption is that the public opinion of the home and immediate community would prove a stronger deterrent and reformative agent than the formal and more impersonal workings of a penal system.

This is a topic as large as the varieties of social suasion and the experience of the human race in their application. It is eminently worthy of research by social scientists, and, so far, little developed. The practice of leaving the punishment to the community has in its favor the point that for any individual the most meaningful punishment is that which is inflicted by those closest to him. It is the opinion of his peers that he values far more than the opinion of some vast and faceless "general public" represented by the sentencing judge. It is a point in its favor, also, that it makes for no discontinuity between the legal and moral community in the way that legal punishment does, in setting off some offences as subject to the sway of jails and jailers while other offences, morally as henious, are not so subject.

There are, on the other hand, serious disadvantages in social suasion as compared to legal punishment. These turn largely around in the concept of "community." In the first place, there can be not only deviant persons, but deviant communities; and where this is so we cannot rely upon the opinion of peers to enforce laws which are for the public good. The deviant community may not regard laws necessary for the well-being of the larger community as incumbent upon it. Perhaps the term "deviant" should not be overstressed. It has inevitable connotations of criminality; and while we wish to include gangs and mobs in these remarks, we wish also to include any community insofar as it pursues its own (supposed) interests to the exclusion of the interests of the larger community, in survival, avoidance of suffering, and enhancement of well-being. If we leave the sanctions of laws designed to further these ends of the larger community up to any smaller community, the system may not be viable, since with respect to the purposes of the laws in question, the smaller community may be deviant. And to rely on the social pressure of the larger community is to weaken the claim of social suasion to operate with the force of the judgment of peers—since the most effective peer-judgment comes from the most immediate communities.

Secondly, were the sanctions left up to the community, the same crime would be punished in many different ways rather than in the one way set by the legal penalty; but this would be unjust. It might be answered that the crime would still be punished in accordance with its seriousness, since in communities where it is a heinous offense it would be punished severely, but where it is only a venal offense it would be punished lightly. But this answer only begs the question, raised in the previous paragraph, whether the smaller community may not be deviant in regarding as venal, *e.g.*, what would be inimical to the well-being of the larger group.

Bearing in mind these reasons for rejecting social suasion as a substitute for punishment, we may without contradiction acknowledge its importance for legal punishment. The force of the threat contained in the penal clause of a criminal law is great not merely because the person contemplating crime fears the pain or suffering the penalty would impose if inflicted. Perhaps it is not even mainly this; for he also greatly fears the judgment of his peers symbolized by this official pronouncement of guilt and sentence. In fact, distinctions are made in everyday life and in legal debate between those penalties (*e.g.* fines) which do not necessarily carry this public disapprobation with them, and those (imprisonment, execution) which do. Justice Brandeis is quoted by Hall[11] as saying, "It is . . . imprisonment in a penitentiary which now renders a crime infamous." But it is a necessary condition of this disapprobation, or infamy, that the criminal has been sentenced to a penitentiary; so the disapprobation is not here to be considered a substitute for punishment.[12]

Let us turn to the practice of rewarding rather than punishing crime. It is not clear how such a practice would operate. Would there be a reward for each person who goes through a year without breaking a law? A reward for each person who, though severely tempted in given circumstances, refrains from violating the law? Such practices are indeed conceivable, but would be subject to grave objections. Those laws which it is most important to enforce are often those there is the greatest temptation to violate. How could we prevent by means of rewards those crimes which in their nature are extremely profitable, such as embezzlement, or forgery? And would the prospect of reward deter a man about to commit a crime of violence? More importantly, would it be morally defensible to reward a person abiding by (presumable necessary and just) laws?

There *is* a sense of the word "reward" in which it is used synonymously with "positive reinforcement." In this sense, reward provides indispensable support for legal punishment. For here reward is indistinguishable from social suasion, the reinforcement in question consisting in the repeated approval of one's abiding by the law under temptation to violate it.

Concerning the possibility of substituting of persuasion for punishment, we would follow Aristotle in his assessment of human nature when he says ". . . most people obey necessity rather than argument, and punishments rather than the sense of what is noble."[13] This should be immediately qualified (as Aristotle qualified it) by our assertion that we would much prefer to use persuasion rather than punishment, since punishment is a practice forced on us by the "human condition" rather than chosen as something positively desirable on its own account. It should also be said that persuasion may have a kind of pyramiding effect with respect to building respect for rules. That is, to the extent that we risk persuasion rather than punishment, we help develop people amenable to persuasion and not needing fear of punishment as a motive for abiding by the rules. Unlike some other alternatives, then, the side-effects of persuasion as a practice are good: better than the side-effects of punishment.

The cause of persuasion is one open to the advocate of punishment, Aristotle's assessment of human nature being granted as a generalization, but not taken to imply that any given person may not change in his amenability to persuasion. Persuasion as a means of encouraging compliance with the laws should clearly be promoted. This means that the rationale of laws should be the subject of public discussion, that only demonstrably necessary or desirable legal rules be enacted, and that some attempt be made to render the body of law intelligible. If persuasion must be rejected, it is not as an adjunct but as a substitute for punishment. And it is not by virtue of its running afoul of the limiting principles that we must reject it as a substitute for punishment, but as failing to measure up to the demands of the guiding principle.

The achievement of a law-abiding community by the use of drugs or Pavlovian conditioning seems in principle perfectly possible, but the side-effects of such procedures we would not, on grounds of humanity, be willing to accept. We would not accept them because they are unnecessarily degrading: unnecessarily, because law-abidingness can be attained at lower cost in human degradation. Thus, as opposed to persuasion, we would accept conditioning so far as the guiding principle is concerned, but reject it for violating the limiting principles.

The case for punishment so far is that, granting certain very general assumptions of fact, the disvalue of misery, and the consequent needs for rules, *a* practice is needed to encourage compliance with rules. And of the alternative practices some (*i.e.,* rewarding, persuading) fail to measure up to the guiding principle as well as punishment, and others (*i.e.,* conditioning, social suasion) are ruled out on the ground that they conflict with justice or humanity. This argument is deficient in two respects. It is not conclusive; since there may be alternatives not taken into account which would compete more successfully with punishment. If this is the case, then it is open to the opponents of punishments to propose these alternatives and compare them to punishment by the criteria of efficiency and acceptability. It is also deficient in that it offers no positive justification of punishment. It says only, so far, that punishment is the least undesirable of the alternatives.

V

There is much to be said for the thesis that punishment is just that: not anything we would want to have in the best of all possible worlds, but something we must accept for lack of something better in the world in which we live. Yet it may be well to note how it measures up to the criteria of efficiency in encouraging compliance with rules, of justice, and of humanity. But before turning to these, we should note that there are some very general assumptions of fact, beyond those which give rise to the need for *a* practice, upon which any justification of the practice of punishment must rest.

The first of these assumptions is that men are capable of calculating their own interest; and that in general they will. Obviously the efficacy of the threat contained in a criminal law rests on this assumption. If a man is unable or unwilling to look ahead to the probable consequences for him of bank robbery then of course the possibility of a prison sentence is no deterrent.

Zilboorg tells us that "The indifference of the criminal to the penalty that is ahead of him, even if this penalty is death, is more the rule than the exception."[14] Bentham, on the other hand, argues

> When matters of such importance as pain and pleasure are at stake, and these in the highest degree (the only matters in short that can be of importance) who is there that does not calculate? Men calculate, some with less exactness, indeed, some with more: but all men calculate. I would not say, that even a mad man does not calculate.[15]

The case seems to me to be overstated on both sides. Bentham does not need to claim that everybody calculates. Even if the percentage of people who calculate is relatively small, punishment would so far be worthwhile; for by the threat of punishment crime could be reduced. And more moderate psychiatrists do not accept such conclusions as Zilboorg's. Robert Waelder, for example, tells us that the claim of "a very small but articulate number of psychiatrists" that punishment does not deter is "a radical contention in view of everybody's daily experience in office and shop."[16]

The second assumption is that, in general, men are able to govern present impulses by the thought of future consequences. If they were not, the threat of punishment would be useless. This, so far as it applies to criminals, is also challenged by some of the more extreme psychiatrists.[17] Third, it is assumed that it is possible to find "evils" which are more or less universally dreaded. If there were no general desire to avoid fines or jail, then these "evils" would not be eligible as punishment. But unless the legislator can find some "evil" which qualifies, the institution of punishment fails; or is modified to allow judges complete discretion in the choice of punishment. Whether this would still be punishment and this "judge" a judge are open questions. Certainly a door would be left ajar for radical abuse of power. There are advocates of the "individualization of punishment" who would be willing to take this risk for the supposed gain in reformatory effectiveness. But what is gained here may well be lost on the side of deterrence of would-be offenders, who could never know what the penalty is, for the crime they contemplate.

To turn to assumptions concerning human society, we assume, first, that there is a virtual monopoly of coercive power in the state. Suppose that each man has an H-bomb which he threatens to explode if molested. Then force could be used on a man only by his consent, and legal punishment would break down. Secondly, we assume that the culture is such that it is possible for people to grasp what it is to be an official in a legal system. If not, sentencing and the execution of sentences will be understood as moves made by particular persons against particular persons; and deterrence will give way to cycles of retaliation. This may help explain why for Tolstoy, who refused on principle to allow the distinction between what is permissible for an official of a system and for an individual falling under the system, punishment was a moral nightmare.

To the extent that any of these assumptions, or the assumptions on which the need for a practice is predicated, are false, the case for legal punishment breaks down. We shall not argue for them, but simply assume their truth. Assuming them true, it seems *a priori* likely that punishment would be effective in encouraging compliance with legal rules. More than this: the experience of centuries of civilization constitutes evidence that it is effective. But not very conclusive evidence. We do not know to what extent social suasion and intellectual conviction have been responsible for the tendency of the masses to abide by the law. We do not have controlled social experiments in which punishment is compared in point of efficacy to treatment, or social suasion, or persuasion. In those chaotic revolutionary situations in which the recent history of the human race abounds, we would hardly have dared rely on less than the strong medicine of legal punishment. Yet perhaps in more orderly times, less drastic practices can be encouraged.

Under the heading of the effectiveness of punishment as a practice we should note (what has sometimes been recognized) that punishment is at least more ingenious than its alternatives in that it works like a pricing system in reverse. Whereas the store keeper tries to price his wares in such a way that there will be as many purchasers as possible; the legislator tries (or should try) to "price" crimes in such a way that there will be as few takers-of-the-risk of criminal behavior as possible. And—as we realize from our survey of Bentham—it is more subtle than this. It is not merely that we want few takers, but that we want less takers of the worst crimes. So on these we put the highest price and our "pricing" can—on the practice of punishment—be carefully adjusted to the disvalue of the crimes: just as (inversely) the storekeeper can progressively encourage the taking of his wares by lowering the price.

What must be borne in mind is that if the evidence for the effectiveness of punishment in encouraging compliance with legal rules is less than satisfactory, the evidence for the comparatively untried alternatives is even less satisfactory. But the burden of proof is on him who would make a change, on the principle that we should change only where there is a likely advantage in doing so. And this principle seems worth defending, since changes, in deep-rooted practices especially, inevitably involve difficult re-adjustments, and sometimes involve consequences not foreseen.

What is also required in justification is that punishment should be shown as acceptable, *i.e.*, as not violating the limiting princi-ples of justice and humanity. Is the practice of punishment, as such, unjust or inhumane? To say that it is, is to say that a person so far uncommitted to a society, recognizing the need in any society for an effective practice to encourage compliance with rules, recognizing that these must be burdens and privileges un-der whatever practice is chosen, would be willing to enter that society and fall under that practice, even though he does not know in advance and from this uncommitted standpoint what role he might have to play and what burdens or privileges would fall to his lot. To say that he would not commit himself to the society on the ground that he might through no fault of his own fall into a role which is at a disadvantage in the distribution of burdens and privileges, receiving, compared to other roles, most of the burdens and none of the privileges, is to say that the prac-tice is unjust. To say that he would not commit himself to the society on the ground that the burdens which must be carried by the players of some roles (even though they may be fairly distributed) are at the same time very heavy and not necessary for the attainment of the purposes of the practice, is to say that the practice is inhumane.

Is the practice of punishment unjust? There is a heavily bur-dened role, criminal, into which any of us might fall; but not, we may assume, without fault. The proper answer to the person who refuses to commit himself to the society containing this practice, on the ground that he might fall into the unfavored role of criminal, is that once he commits himself to society and prac-tice, whether he then plays or avoids the role of criminal is still open. He *can* have the advantages of the practice, and at the same time avoid the burdens of the unfavored role. And should he fall into the role of criminal, there is nothing inherent in the practice which would make the burden borne by one category of criminal out of proportion to that borne by others, granted the need to distinguish between more and less dangerous crimes.

Is it inhumane? Since, as practice, it does not specify the bur-dens to be borne, but only that they shall be adequate to the purpose of discouraging crime, the practice does not *as such* demand that there should be burdens not warranted by its purpose. It does not follow from the fact that there may be "cruel and unusual" punishments that the practice of punishment is therefore inhumane. Contrast the practice whereby the rulers administer drugs to the population at large which ensure that whatever laws are enacted will not be violated. This could work only if the critical faculties were so deadened that the individual could no longer distinguish between good and bad laws, and between occasions on which even good laws should and should not be violated. But, since there are alternative ways of encouraging compliance with the laws, which do not involve these consequences, they are unnecessary, and the practice is inhumane.

Morally speaking, if our very general assumptions of fact be granted, and our judgment that widespread misery is a disvalue, then rules are necessary, and some way must be found to make them effective. But if the best and most acceptable way is the practice of legal punishment, then those persons who find themselves playing the roles of judge and jailer have the moral right to sentence and carry out sentences. They have this right as officials of a practice which is, by hypothesis, for the good of everyone alike.

VI

So much, then, for the justification of the practice of legal punishment. It may be well to point out some things this justification does *not* pretend to do. 1) It does not pretend to offer a conclusive argument for punishment, whatever that would be. It presents the case for punishment: a case which must be compared with the case which can be made out for available alternative practices. 2) It does not, as we have noted, claim to warrant punishment as preferable to other practices regardless of context. It could well be that, for example, in a simple, stable, closely interdependent society, where there is more emphasis on character than on rules, punishment would be out of place. 3) It does not justify any particular mode of punishment, such as capital punishment or imprisonment.

The objection that capital punishment or imprisonment are inhumane does not, even if accepted, necessarily weigh against the practice of legal punishment; since there are other modes of punishment which can be used. However, there is a finite number of modes, and if we were unable to find effective and acceptable modes, this would undercut the case for legal punishment.

The argument over capital punishment tends to turn in the wrong gimbals. Even if it should be shown that capital punishment is more effective than some other mode of punishment in discouraging certain sorts of crime, this would not be sufficient to justify its use; for it might be ruled out as acceptable by justice or humanity as limiting principles. So far as justice is concerned, capital punishment can be as impartially administered as any other mode of punishment. It is argued, with great force, that it is not in fact impartially administered, and that those executed tend to be the poor and the ignorant. This would not make any great difference, unfortunately, between capital punishment and imprisonment, were it not for the important point that there is no way of rectifying a judicial error arising from inadequate legal representation, once a man has been executed. Since there is the possibility of an irreversible error stemming from inadequate representation, it seems clear that our uncommitted individual, contemplating societies with varying modes of punishment, and not knowing whether he would play the role of rich or poor man, should he join the society, would prefer a society which did not have capital punishment to one which did. On this test, capital punishment is unjust.

But the capital punishment society may fail the test of humanity as well. For if our uncommitted onlooker can see no clear case for the thesis that capital punishment is necessary for the encouragement of compliance with the law, and is aware of alternative less cruel modes of punishment which singly or together are as effective, then he will naturally avoid the capital punishment society, even though he may think sentences to capital punishment are nondiscriminatory. And this much is clear: that no clear-cut case showing the necessity of capital punishment as a means of discouraging crime has been brought forward.

It might be argued that it is an unfair burden of proof to place upon the advocate of capital punishment to require him to show that his mode of punishment is necessary for the discouragement of crime, whereas the same burden is not placed upon the advocates of imprisonment and fines. But the difference is that capital punishment is admittedly more cruel than imprisonment[18] and fines and therefore should, upon the principle of humanity, be ruled out if it can be dispensed with. And, we may add, there is ample evidence that capital punishment can be abolished without an advance in the rate of crimes it purportedly discouraged.

There are some persons who argue that life imprisonment is more cruel than capital punishment, and there is much to be said for this thesis, but there seems to be no way of deciding *in general* which is more cruel. Our test would have to be the same; namely to ask ourselves whether an uncommitted outsider would choose a capital punishment society in preference to a life-imprisonment society. And (granting for the moment that "life-imprisonment" really means imprisonment for life) we cannot be certain how he would answer, since we do not know whether he would be young or old, well or ill, disdainful or not of the prudent preservation of mere existence. However, the choice fortunately does not have to be made, since the sentence of life imprisonment today rarely means that in fact the criminal will remain in prison for the rest of his life.[19]

What, then, of imprisonment as a punishment? The live question here is not whether imprisonment, which unlike capital punishment admits of degrees, is justifiable, but what kind and how much imprisonment is justifiable. What has not been sufficiently recognized by the general public, in spite of the writings of G.B. Shaw,[20] Galsworthy,[21] John Barlow Martin[22] and others is that imprisonment can be a kind of torture worse than mutilation or the rack. Whether it is will depend upon the conditions and duration of imprisonment, and, inevitably, upon the character and personality of the offender. It is clear that from the standpoint of justice and humanity, to say nothing of efficiency, imprisonment as a mode of punishment should receive careful scrutiny. It is by and large only by the latter criterion that it tends to be measured. Here the argument sometimes slides from the inefficiency of a given penitentiary system to the undesirability of imprisonment as a mode of punishment (or even to the undesirablity of punishment as a practice.) Yet it does not follow that because a given mode of imprisonment is inefficient that imprisonment as a mode of punishment is inefficient; and, since efficiency is a comparative criterion, it must be shown that there are more efficient modes of punishment which can replace imprisonment. And of course even if imprisonment were the most efficient mode of punishment available, it would not follow that, by the same token, it should be accepted.

The careful scrutiny of imprisonment as a mode of punishment not only from the standpoint of efficiency (here excellent work has already been done) but also of humanity and justice would result, I believe, in a radical reappraisal of the conditions and duration of imprisonment: in bold experiments, at least, in the shortening of legal penalties. For without such probing experiments the burden of proof, which humanity requires, that the penalties presently in force are necessary for the discouragement of crime, will not have been shouldered.

What we say here implies, correctly, that we believe that the schema of guiding and limiting principles can be applied not only to the justification of the practice of punishment but also to the justification of penal legislation. This we will not undertake here, but the main lines of the venture should be clear. Here the questions would be, first, whether a law is necessary, and, second, whether the proposed law would be the most efficient of the acceptable alternatives. But justice and humanity as limiting principles of legislation cannot be defined or applied in the same way as they are above. The uncommitted bystander must have committed himself to the practice of punishment, and must now consider alternative laws under that practice. Should we then attempt to apply our schema to the justification of sentences? If so, our uncommitted bystander must have accepted not only the practice but the law violated, along with its attached range of penalties.

Whether the distinction between guiding and limiting principles can be maintained in the justification of sentences is a difficult question not to be undertaken here. It is enough, for our purposes, if the conclusion of Chapter IV be allowed to stand: that the judge cannot be reduced either to a social engineer, or to a balancer of the scales.

The short answer to Tolstoy's question, "By what right do some people punish others?" is that, needing a practice, we do not know any better one than legal punishment. The long answer would begin with this chapter and move back to the justification of legislation, penalties, and sentences. This book may provide an outline and some material for that venture.

CHAPTER VII

FOOTNOTES

1. We will settle here on the wider term, "practice," since we wish to compare punishment with possible alternatives which would qualify as practices but not as institutions.

2. "Justification," in general, is discussed in Chapter VI.

3. The general view of the justification of punishment presented here is perhaps closer to Ross' than to any other traditional view. The distinctions made here, however, give us certain advantages over Ross' account. Ross speaks of the balance between the *prima facie* duty of "injuring wrong-doers only to the extent that they have injured others," and the *prima facie* duty of "promoting the general interest." (*The Right and The Good*, Oxford, 1930, Ch. II, Appendix II, "Punishment"). In the first place, our account avoids the implication that we simply balance these considerations one against the other like weights on a scale (*op. cit.*, pp. 63 and 41). It is not a question of choosing either justice or utility or a balance between, but of finding the most useful social device consistent with the demands of justice. Secondly (though Ross might well not agree that this is an advantage) the emphasis is more on standing on, or holding a principle, than on knowing that something is true. Third, our account is not open, as Ross' is, to the kind of objection raised by J. S. Mill (in *Hamilton*) to the effect that we cannot very well balance the maxims of justice against those of utility, since what one maxim of justice demands may be incompatible with what another maxim of justice demands. On the present account, such conflicts, which I believe are real, need not concern us; since if the practice in question conflicts with any maxim which we adhere to, then it is ruled out; and we must look about for one which is acceptable. But, like Ross, we are able to avoid the charge that, by setting in motion an utilitarian engine of justification uncurbed, we are likely to justify too much.

4. The term is used here in the broad sense explained in Chapter V.

5. How many limiting principles are there? This is like asking how many ways there are for an effective practice to go awry. Limiting principles reject the proposed practice because it can be seen in advance that once this device is set in motion there are ways in which it would operate which we could never accept. But because the demand for *a* practice is sometimes very great, the grounds on which a candidate may be ruled out as nonacceptable are naturally very much curtailed. Justice and humanity, in that order, seem to be the limiting principles which bind with the greatest stringency; but for less important practice-choices, many more limiting principles can enter in. Compare the choice of a practice for assigning responsibility for the rearing of the young, to the choice of a practice by which recipients of the "keys of the city" are to be designated.

6. The definition of and test for justice in a practice are topics which lead way beyond the scope of the present discussion. What is offered here is merely an approach which seems to me promising. One might agree that justice is a limiting principle even though one disagreed that it could be defined as it is defined here. Much of what I have to say here has been suggested by John Rawls' article, "Justice as Fairness" (*Philosophical Review*, 1958, pp. 164-194). For a more complete discussion, the reader is referred to the whole of this article. I do not adopt Rawls' device of positing that the uncommitted individual we must picture is completely self-interested. He is but a construct, and we can do with him what we please, but to require that he be merely self-interested is to risk misleading comparison with Hobbes, and to make him more artificial than is necessary for my purpose. His recognition that *a* practice is needed may be based in part on altruism:

a regard for the well-being of (even remote) others. But he would not likely join that society which would not give him, or anyone, a fair shake.

7. Compare "burdened" and "prilvileged" vessels in the International Rules of the Road.

8. This, of course, is over-simple. The quarrels in question often arose out of supposed insults which, according to the code of honor, could only be expunged by duelling; so that it was the code of honor as a whole which had to give way, not duelling alone.

9. The discussion here is, admittedly, barely opened. How, by what test, do we decide that degradation, misery, or death are *unnecessary?* And, even more difficult, what is to *count as* misery, suffering, and (most difficult) degradation? But even though the theoretical explication of our test for humanity of a practice may be difficult, still the test can be used prior to explication; for, by and large and never-mind-how, we do agree on what is unnecessary, and on whether suffering, misery, and degradation (to say nothing of death) are imposed. Or, if we do not agree, we know how to go about discussing the point. Explication could only start from the considerations we take as relevant in such discussion.

10. Justice may be thought of as a virtue of practices, or actions, or of men. If we start from justice as a virtue of practices we will tend to think of acts and men as just insofar as they conform to the practices; and if we start from justice as a virture of acts we will tend to think of practices as just insofar as they require the kinds of acts which we already, prior to the practice, consider just. But there is something odd in the notion that there can be justice of actions prior to justice of practices (though there is nothing odd about the notion of justice of actions prior to justice of institutions), and that the justice of practices consists in making these, prior, just actions possible. Does punishment, as a practice, exist to make possible that balance of punishment and desert which is known, independently of the practice, to be what justice demands? This is not at all plausible if we think in wide, generic, terms of the "practice of punishment." It becomes more plausible as we confine ourselves to particular practices or those formal practices we call institutions.

11. *Op. cit.,* p. 327.

12. The question, presently much discussed, whether or not a given piece of legislation is punitive in intent, is likely to turn on the question not merely what suffering it imposes but also on the way in which the suffering is imposed will be generally regarded. A suggested test for legislation punitive in intent is to determine "whether the legislative concern underlying the statute was to regulate 'the activity or status from which the individual is barred' or whether the statute is evidently 'aimed at the person or class or persons disqualified' ". (Fleming *v.* Nestor, 363 U.S. 603 (1960)).

13. *Ethica Nichomachea,* 118a, 3-13.

14. Gregory Zilboorg, *The Psychology of the Criminal Act and Punishment,* New York, 1954, p. 32.

15. *Principles of Morals and Legislation,* XIV, 28.

16. "Psychiatry and the Problem of Criminal Responsibility," *University of Pennsylvania Law Review,* 1952, p. 383.

17. Cf., *e.g.,* Karpman's definition of criminal behavior, p. 102.

18. See qualifications below.

19. "Life Imprisonment means, on the average, only about ten years." (H. E. Barnes and N. K. Teeters, *New Horizons in Criminology,* 3rd ed., Englewood Cliffs, N. J., 1959, p. 59).

20. *Imprisonment,* New York, 1924.

21. John Galsworthy, *The Silver Box,* New York & London, 1909; and *Justice,* New York, 1913.

22. "Prison: The Enemy of Society," *Harpers,* April, 1954, pp. 29-38; and many other articles and books.

A SELECTED BIBLIOGRAPHY

This is a list of some articles and books not mentioned in the text but nevertheless worthy of mention. The psychiatric, sociological, and legal literature is vast; the writings listed here and in the notes may provide beginning-points for the interested reader. For additional articles and books on the philosophical problems of punishment, published in this century, see the bibliography for Chapter X of *Freedom and Responsibility: Readings in Philosophy and Law*. Herbert Morris, ed., Stanford, California 1961.

1. ABRAHAMSEN, DAVID, *Crime and the Human Mind*, New York, 1944. *Cf.* especially Chapters II, IX, and X. A well-balanced, simply written presentation of the issues between psychiatrists and lawyers. The underlying philosophical issues are not discussed.
2. ALEXANDER, FRANZ and STAUB, H., *The Criminal, The Judge, and the Public*, G. Zilboorg (translator), New York, 1931. A moderate psychiatric approach. Not all criminals are mentally deranged.
3. ARISTOTLE, *Ethica Nichomachea*, 1104b, 15-19. Punishment is a "kind of cure." 1180a, 1-13. Punishment is appropriate for those of "inferior nature" who cannot be urged "by the motive of the noble."
4. ARISTOTLE, *Politics*, VII, xiii, 6-7. Criminal and distributive justice contrasted. The former is "forced on the agent," and "has value only as a necessity."
5. ASCOLI, MAX, "Far More Than Chessman," *Reporter*, April 14, 1960, Editorial. The theory that the trial itself, as a "stylized re-enactment of the crime," serves to "purge" society of the crime.
6. BRANHAM, V. C., and KUTASH, S. B., *Encyclopedia of Criminology*, New York, 1949. The quality of the articles is spotty, but there are useful bibliographies and articles by such well-known figures as the Gluecks, Robert Linder, Winfred Overholser, E. H. Sutherland, and G. Zilboorg.
7. CARRITT, E. F., *Ethical and Political Thinking*, Oxford, 1947, Chapter V, "Punishment and Reward." Some difficulties in the traditional theories surveyed.
8. DE TARDE, GABRIEL, *Penal Philosophy*, Boston, 1916, Edward Lindsey (translator). *Cf.* especially all of Section 90, on punishment as a pricing system.
9. DURKEIM, EMILE, *The Division of Labor in Society*, George Simpson (translator), Glencoe, Illinois, 1947, *Cf.* especially Volume I, Chapter 2, Section 2; and Appendix III. The role of punishment in culture.
10. ELLIOT, MABEL A., *Conflicting Penal Theories in Statutory Criminal Law*, 1931. An elementary guide to the main lines of discussion between psychologists, psychiatrists, criminologists, and lawyers about the purposes and methods of criminal law.
11. EWING, A. C., "Punishment as Viewed by The Philosopher," *Canadian Bar Review*, XXI (1942), 91-122. Prof. Ewing's book, *The Morality of*

Punishment, though but mentioned in the text, is the most important single philosophical work on the subject published in this century.

12. FLETCHER, JOSEPH F., "The Ethics of Criminal Guilt"—*Social Meaning of Legal Concepts—No. 2, Criminal Guilt,* New York University School of Law, New York, 1950, 171-184. An argument against the theories that "crimes are not imputable but only punishable for the sake of deterrance, expiation, reformation, or vindication of the law" and that "there is no crime except crime against the state."

13. GALLIE, W. B., "The Lords' Debate on Hanging, July, 1956: Interpretation and Comment," *Philosophy,* 1957, 132-47. Suggests a different classification of the positions than the usual retributivist-utilitarian one.

14. GLUECK, SHELDON, and GLUECK, ELEANOR, *After-Conduct of Discharged Offenders,* London, 1945. Summarizes the results of the Glueck's influential research. Even well-run juvenile courts and reformatories fail to reform any appreciable number of juvenile offenders.

15. GREEN, T. H., *Lectures on the Principles of Political Obligation,* London, 1941, 180-205. Every man has a right to "free life," which right in turn rests on "the assumed capacity in every man of free action contributory to the social good. . . . This . . . implies the right . . . to prevent such actions as interfere with the possibility of free action contributory to the social good."

16. HODGES, D. C. "Punishment," *Philosophy and Phenomenological Research,* 1957, 209-218.

17. KAUFMAN, ARNOLD S., "The Reform Theory of Punishment," *Ethics,* October 1960, 49-53. The justification of punishment as leading to reform is morally suspect, involving conflict with other more important moral beliefs.

18. LLEWELLYN, KARL N., "The Anthropology of Criminal Guilt" in *Social Meaning of Legal Concepts, No. 2, Criminal Guilt,* New York University School of Law, New York, 1950. Distinguishes between an "arms-length" (ours) and "parental" (preferable to ours) system of criminal law. On the first, the offender is disposed of according to the outcome of a game played by two professional adversaries according to strict rules. On the second, the culprit is one of the in-group who has gone wrong, and it is up to everyone to find out what the trouble is and get him "back on the track."

19. MACLAGLAN, W. G., "Punishment and Retribution," *Philosophy,* 1939, 281-298.

20. McCLOSKEY, H. J., "The Complexity of the Concepts of Punishment," *Philosophy,* October 1962, 307-325. Denies that any general theory of punishment is possible because there are radically different punishment-practices, and no one of these is "core" or "basic" to the others. Punishment may be undeserved and should not be defined in such a way as to make desert built in.

21. McCONNELL, RAY M., *Criminal Responsibility and Social Restraint.* New York, 1912. There is a useful discussion of the *lex talionis* on pp. 22-59.

22. MICHAEL, J., and ADLER M., *Crime, Law, and Social Science*, New York, 1933, *Cf.* especially Parts I and III.

23. MICHAEL, J., and WECHSLER, H., *Criminal Law and its Administration*, Chicago, 1950. *Cf.* especially I, 2 ("The Basic Problems of Criminal Law; Ends and Means"). The appendices containing various criminal codes are useful as source-material. *Cf.* also, Parts III, and IV.

24. NOWELL-SMITH, P. H. *Ethics*, London, 1954. The distinction is made between the "Judge's problem" and the "Legislator's problem" in Chapter 19, but is not elaborated.

25. NOWELL-SMITH, P. H. "Freewill and Moral Responsibility," *Mind*, 45-61. Emphasizes the relation between retributive theory of punishment and belief in a God who will retaliate unless actions offensive to him are expiated.

26. PLATO, *Protagoras*, 324-325: The purpose of punishment. *Gorgias*, 479-80: Punishment a painful cure; 525-526: The "proper office" of punishment, *Republic*, 380: Punishment a benefit; *Laws*, V, 735-6: Punishment a purification; IX, 853: Penal legislation "in a manner disgraceful."

27. PRICE, RICHARD, *A Review of The Principal Questions in Morals*, D. Daiches Raphael (ed), first published in 1758, present edition, Oxford, 1948. Argues ingeniously that the rightness or wrongness of punishment cannot depend solely on utility, and may be directly intuited without regard to consequences.

28. RASHDALL, H., *The Theory of Good and Evil*, 2nd Edition. London, 1924, Volume I, Chapter IX, "Punishment and Forgiveness."

29. STROMBERG, TORE, "Some Reflections on the Concept of Punishment," *Theoria*, 1956, 71-83. Examination of the notion of "abolishing" punishment.

30. WHITE, WILLIAM A., *Crimes and Criminals*, New York 1933, *Cf.* especially Chapter XI for the argument that punishment does positive harm and should be replaced by treatment.

INDEX OF NAMES